The Nation's #1 Educational Publisher

McGraw·Hill Learning Materials

SPECTRUM SPELLING

KRAFFT

Grade 1

Author

Nancy Roser
Professor, Language and Literacy Studies
Department of Curriculum and Instruction
The University of Texas at Austin

8787 Orion Place
Columbus, OH 43240-4027

The **McGraw·Hill** Companies

Credits

Illustrations: Olivia Cole, Steve McInturff, Sherry Neidigh, Sue Parnell
Heads: John Kurtz

McGraw-Hill
Consumer Products
A Division of The McGraw-Hill Companies

Copyright © 1998 McGraw-Hill Consumer Products.
Published by McGraw-Hill Learning Materials, an imprint of
McGraw-Hill Consumer Products.

Printed in the United States of America. All rights reserved.
Except as permitted under the United States Copyright Act, no part
of this publication may be reproduced or distributed in any form or
by any means, or stored in a database or retrieval system, without
prior written permission from the publisher.

Send all inquiries to:
McGraw-Hill Learning Materials
8787 Orion Place
Columbus, OH 43240-4027

ISBN 1-57768-161-4

How to Study a Word

1 **Look** at the word.

   What does it mean?
   How is it spelled?

   print

2 **Say** the word.

   What sounds do you hear?
   Are there any silent letters?

   print

3 **Think** about the word.

   How is each sound spelled?
   Do you see any word parts?

   pr i nt

4 **Write** the word.

   Did you copy all the letters carefully?
   Did you think about the sounds
   and letters?

   print

5 **Check** the spelling.

   Did you spell the word correctly?
   Do you need to write it again?

   print

Contents

Lesson		Page
1	Things I Take to School	6
2	Who's at the Zoo?	10
3	Home at Night	14
4	My Top Ten Animals	18
5	What Animals Do for Food	22
6	Being at Home	26
7	Going on Vacation	30
8	Winter Treats	34
9	Driving My Tub	38
10	I Won!	42
11	Play Ball!	46
12	Fox and Box	50
13	My Trunk on the Truck	54
14	My Desk at School	58
15	What's for Dinner?	62
16	A Wonderful Pet	66
17	Dad Ran	70
18	Hop on Top	74

19	Run in the Sun	78
20	A Pet Hen	82
21	Did Pig Win?	86
22	Club Flip Flop	90
23	You Are You	94
24	Review	98
25	Make and Bake	102
26	Notes on Bone	106
27	See Me Weed	110
28	Bike Ride Time	114
29	Day of Rain	118
30	Review	122
31	Stop for the Snake	126
32	This Chat	130
33	Which Ship	134
34	They Have Come	138
35	Green Yellow Red	142
36	Review	146
Speller's Handbook		151
Speller Dictionary		157

1 Things I Take To School

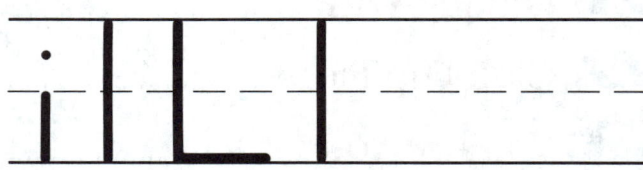

xzyz

Ring the letters that are the same.

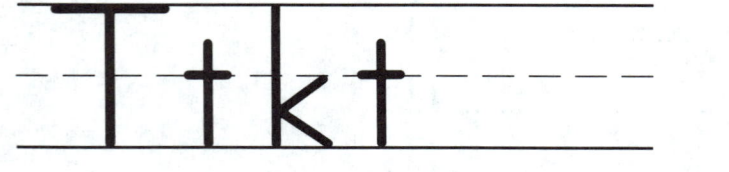

kXKK

TItI

YZZz

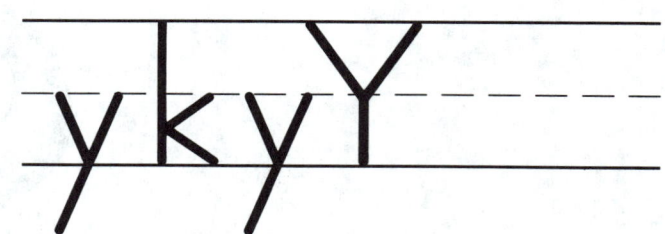

Name the letter.
Trace the letter.
Write the letter.

Lesson 1 7

Name the letter.
Trace the letter.
Write the letter.

8   Lesson 1

Name the letter.
Trace the letter.
Write the letter.

V V

v v

W W

w w

X X

x x

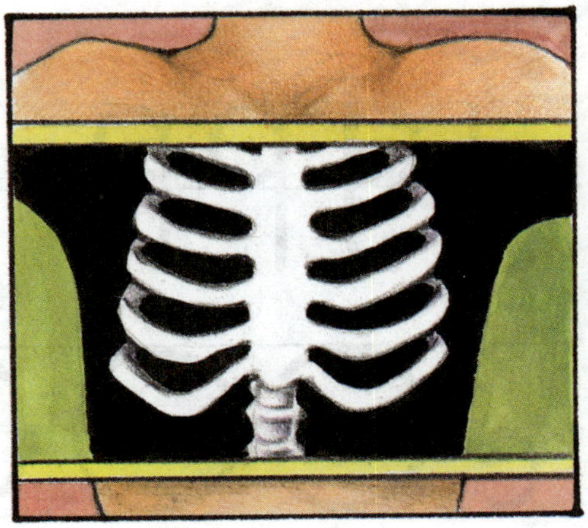

Lesson 1

2 Who's at the Zoo?

Ring the letters that are the same.

U O u U

s s c o

P B D P

B d b d

J G g J

j g p p

O u U O

c C O C

d b b p

Lesson 2

Name the letter.
Trace the letter.
Write the letter.

Lesson 2   11

Name the letter.
Trace the letter.
Write the letter.

S S

s s

J J

j j

G G

g g

12 Lesson 2

Name the letter.
Trace the letter.
Write the letter.

P P

p p

B B

b b

D D

d d

Lesson 2

3 Home at Night

Ring the letters that are the same.

m M n m

a e A a

E F e E

H N N M

f F h h

r r R F

Q Q E F

f r R f

a q e q

14   Lesson 3

Name the letter.
Trace the letter.
Write the letter.

Lesson 3   15

Name the letter.
Trace the letter.
Write the letter.

A A

a a

E E

e e

Q Q

q q

16 Lesson 3

Name the letter.
Trace the letter.
Write the letter.

Ff Rr Oo Mm

Lesson 3 17

4
My Top Ten Animals

Name the pictures.
Match the beginning sounds.

18 Lesson 4

Name the picture.
Ring the beginning letter.

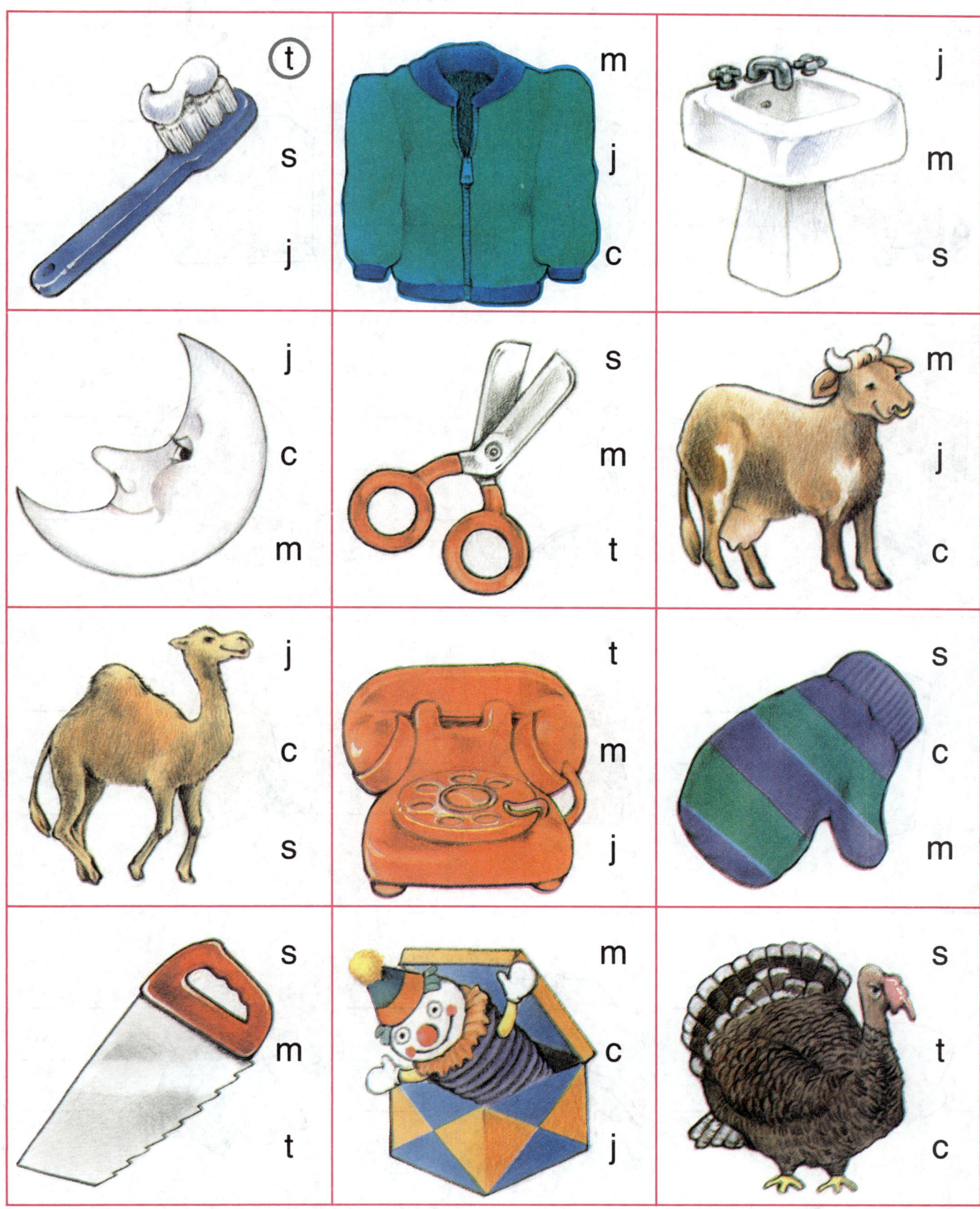

Lesson 4

Name the picture.
Write the beginning letter.

c		

20 Lesson 4

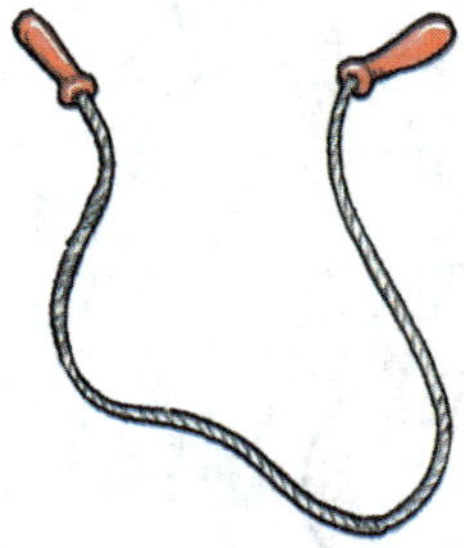

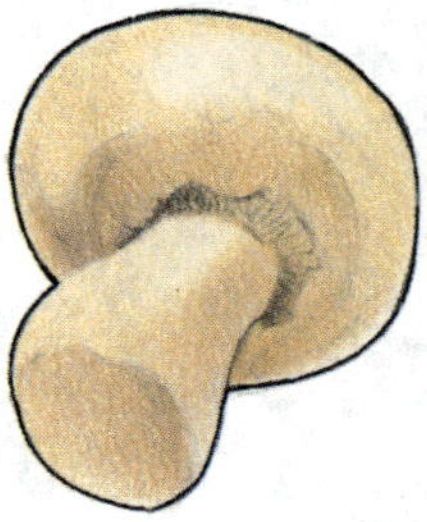

Name the picture.
Write the beginning letter.

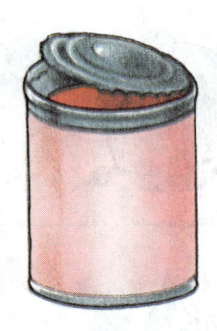 _can

 _ar

 _op

 _op

 _up

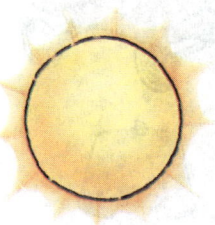 _un

Lesson 4   21

5
What Animals Do for Food

Name the pictures.
Match the beginning sounds.

22 Lesson 5

Name the picture.
Ring the beginning letter.

Lesson 5   23

Name the picture.
Write the beginning letter.

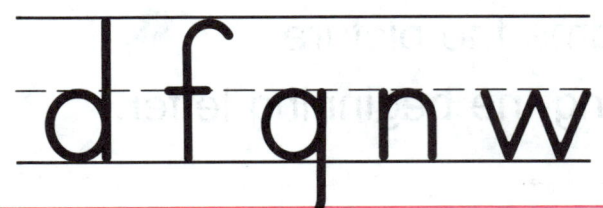

d _d_

g ___

w ___

n ___

n ___

d ___

g ___

n ___

f ___

d ___

w ___

n ___

24   Lesson 5

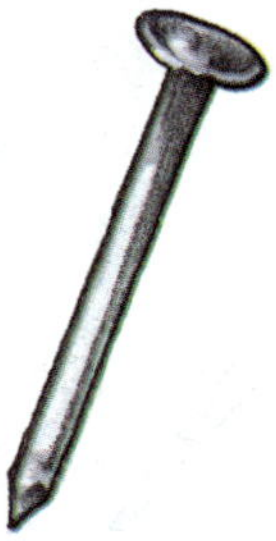

Name the picture.
Write the beginning letter.

d f g n w

 nut

 og

 ig

 ox

 as

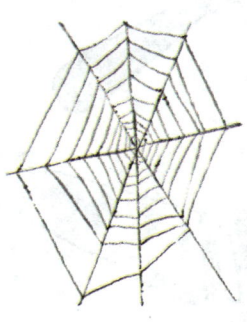 eb

6 Being at Home

Name the pictures.
Match the beginning sounds.

26 Lesson 6

Name the picture.
Ring the beginning letter.

house — b (h) p	ring — r b h	parachute — p r b
bike — h p b	heart — r p h	butterfly — b r p
helicopter — h b r	pen — p h b	rainbow — h r b
bell — b p h	rake — p r b	pot — h b p

Lesson 6

Name the picture.
Write the beginning letter.

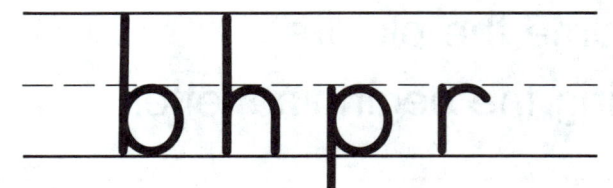

b h p r

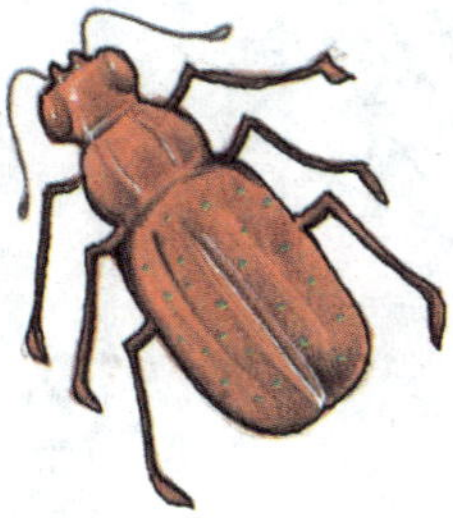

b

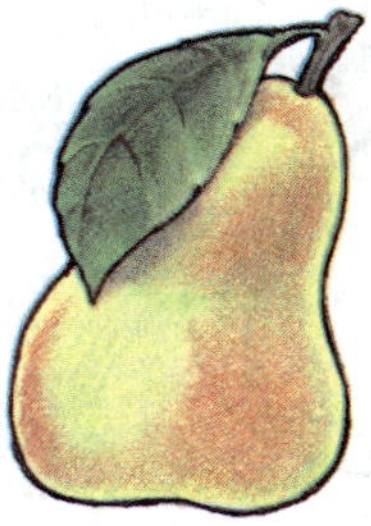

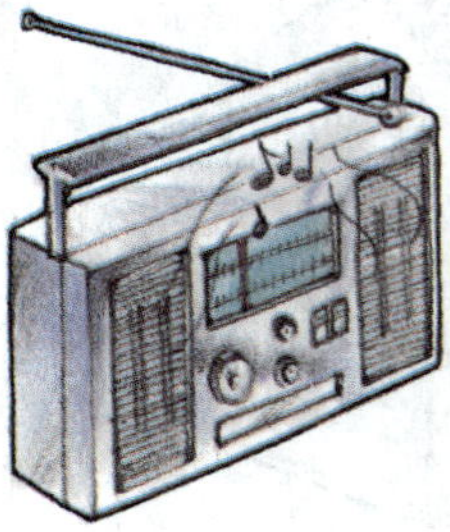

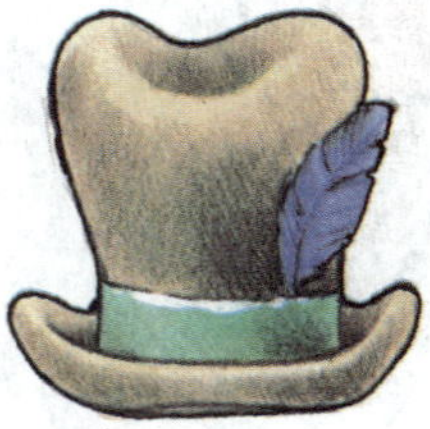

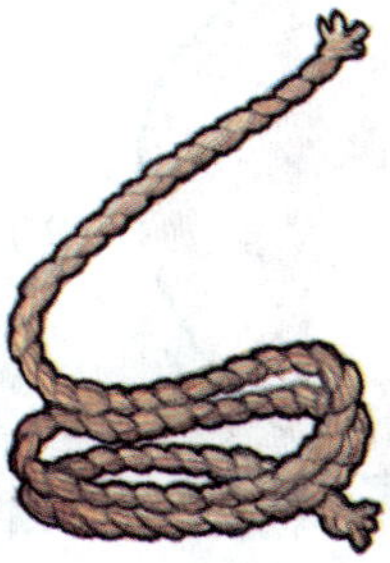

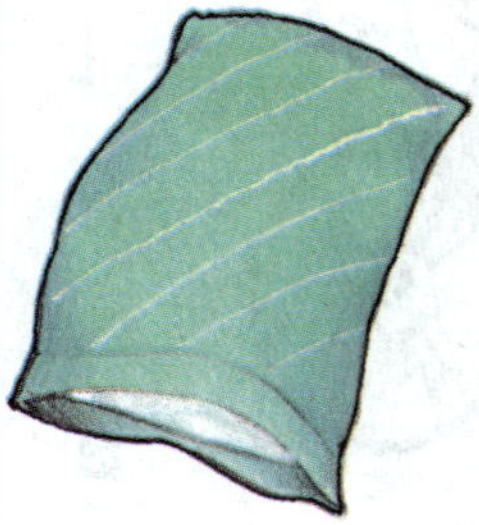

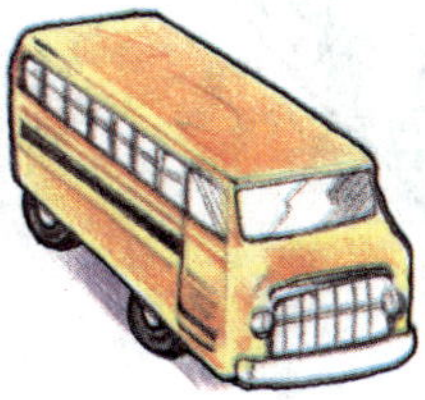

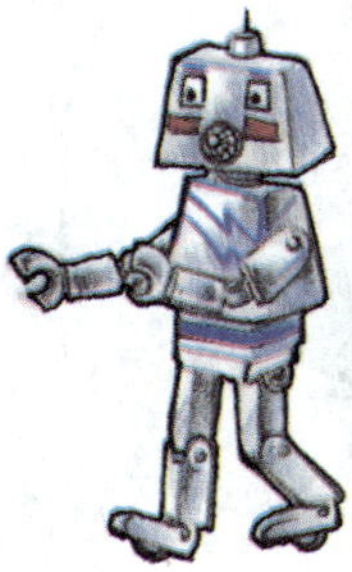

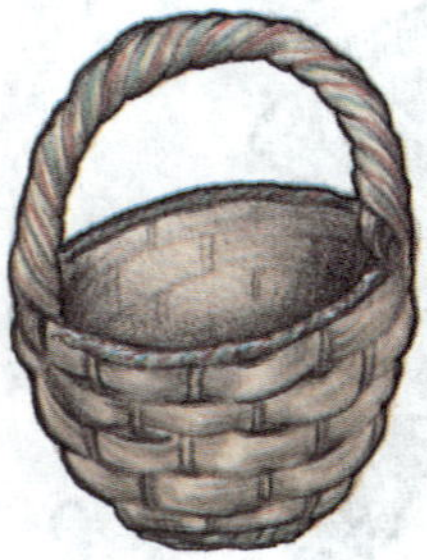

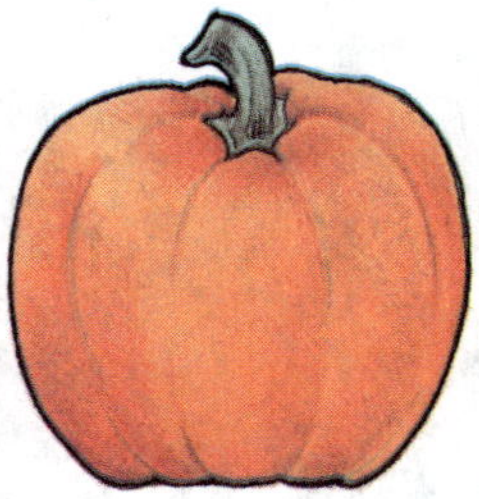

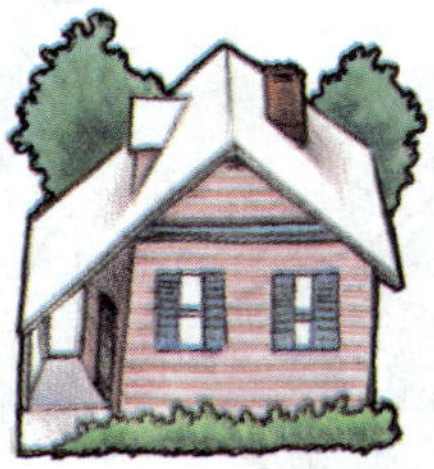

Name the picture.
Write the beginning letter.

 hen

 ot

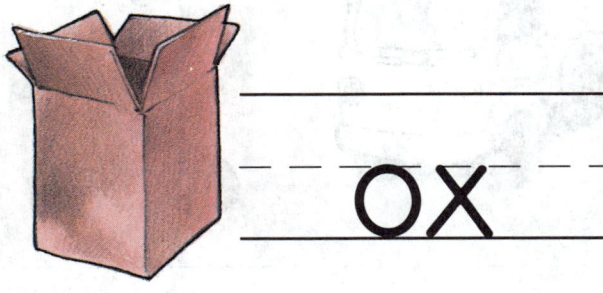 ox

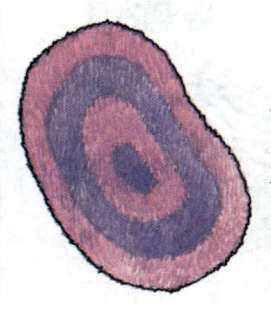 ug

 ed

 at

7 Going on Vacation

Name the pictures.
Match the beginning sounds.

Lesson 7

Name the picture.
Ring the beginning letter.

Lesson 7

Name the picture.
Write the beginning letter.

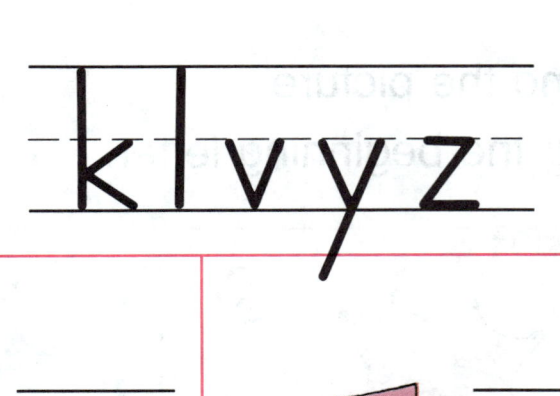

32 Lesson 7

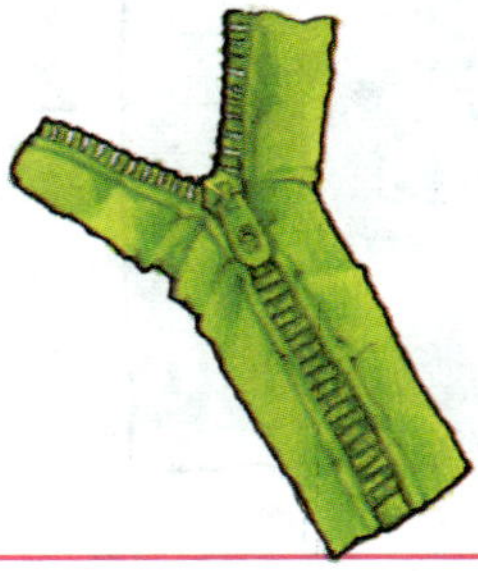

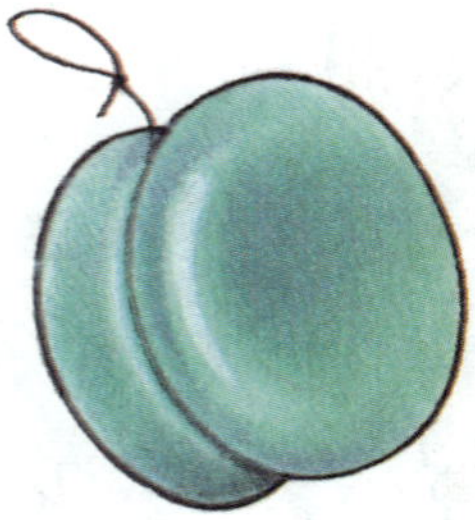

Name the picture.
Write the beginning letter.

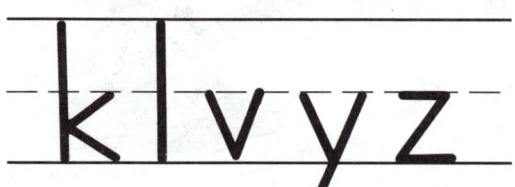

 yak

 iss

 id

 an

 oo

 og

Lesson 7

8 Winter Treats

Name the pictures.
Match the ending sounds.

Lesson 8

Name the picture.
Ring the ending letter.

Lesson 8

Name the picture.
Write the ending letter.

36 Lesson 8

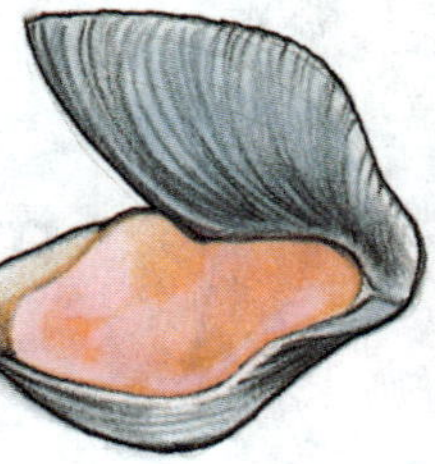

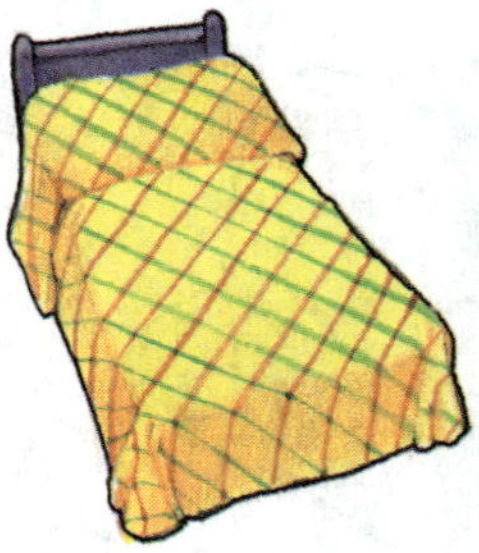

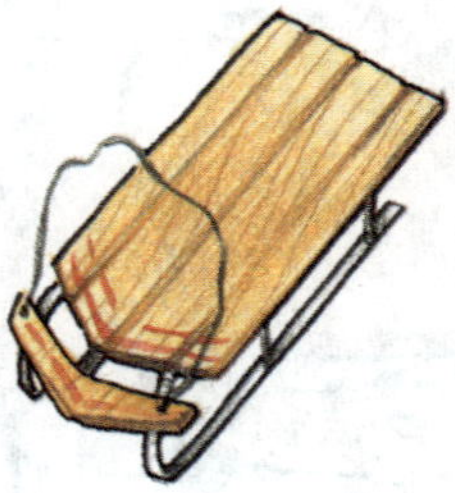

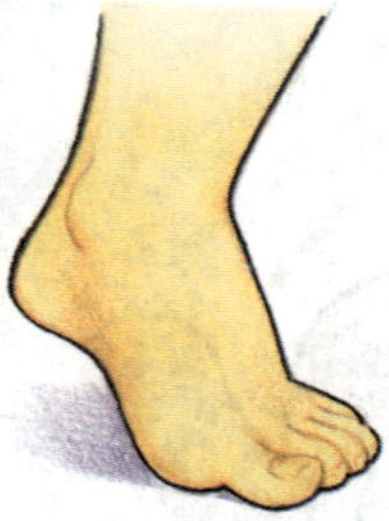

Name the picture.
Write the ending letter.

jam

pa_

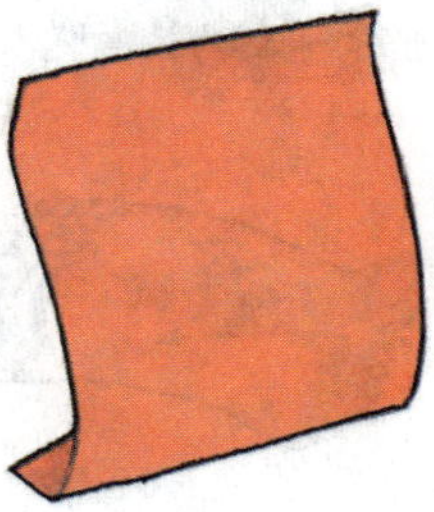

re_

ca_

mo_

je_

Lesson 8

9 Driving My Tub

Name the pictures.
Match the ending sounds.

Name the picture.
Ring the ending letter.

Lesson 9

Name the picture.
Write the ending letter.

frog — g	crab — ___	pig — ___
crib — ___	glass — ___	mug — ___
bib — ___	flag — ___	tub — ___
bus — ___	dog — ___	egg — ___

40   Lesson 9

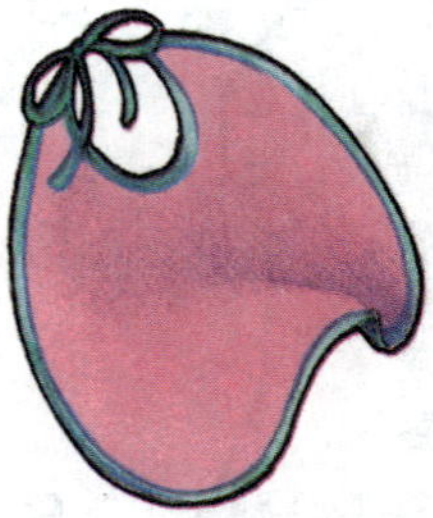

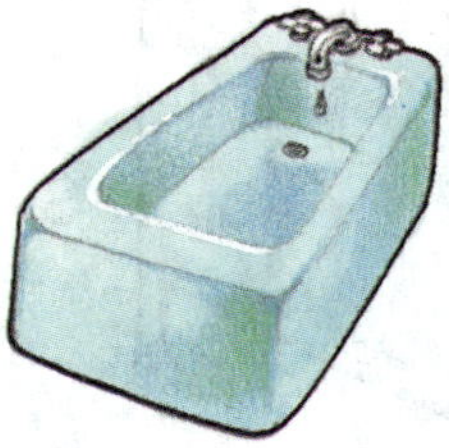

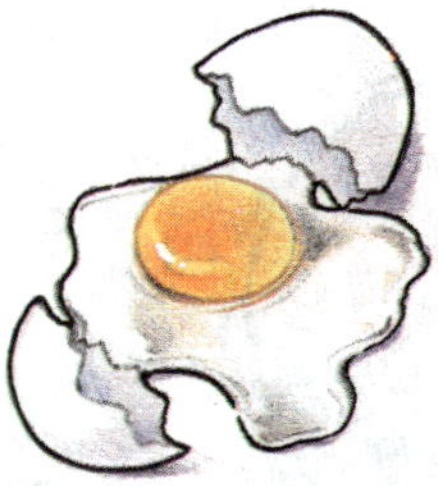

Name the picture.
Write the ending letter.

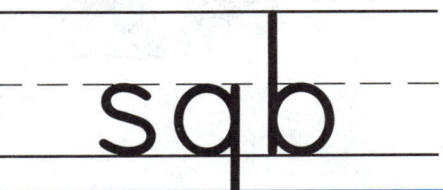
s g b

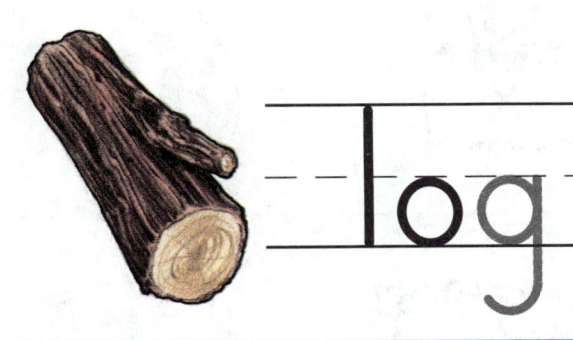
log

ga

bi

bu

bu

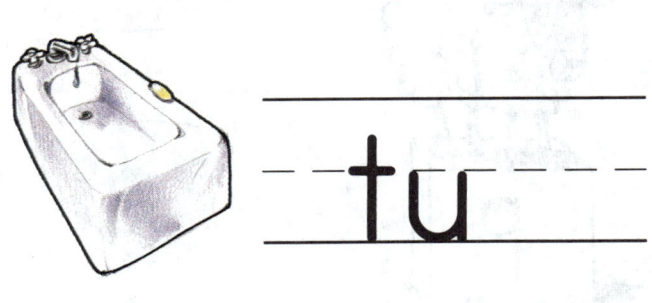
tu

Lesson 9

10
I Won!

Name the pictures.
Match the ending sounds.

42 Lesson 10

Name the picture.
Ring the ending letter.

Lesson 10

Name the picture.
Write the ending letter.

pnx

44 Lesson 10

Name the picture.
Write the ending letter.

pnx

 van

 bo___

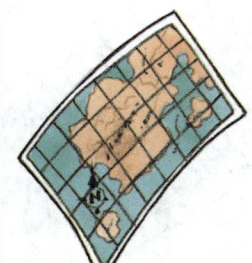 ma___

 si___

 cu___

 pa___

Lesson 10

11 Play Ball!

Ring the pictures with the same middle sound as  cat

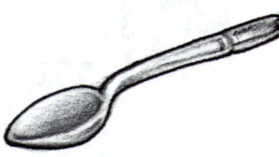
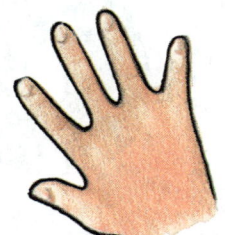

Match the middle sounds.

Lesson 11

Name the picture.
Listen for the short *a* sound.
Write the letter *a*.

48 Lesson 11

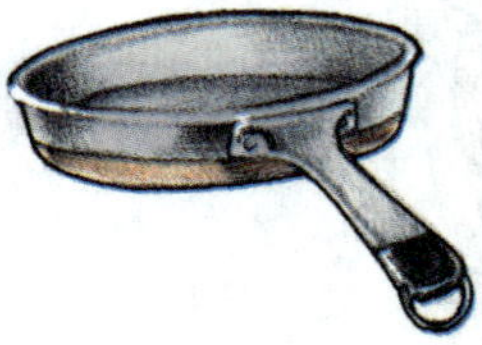

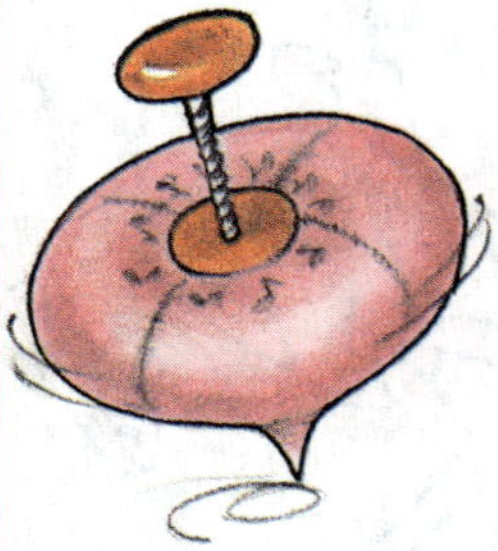

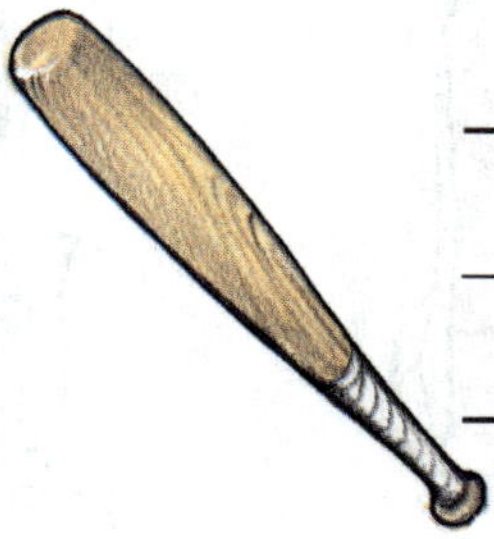

Name the picture.
Write the letter.

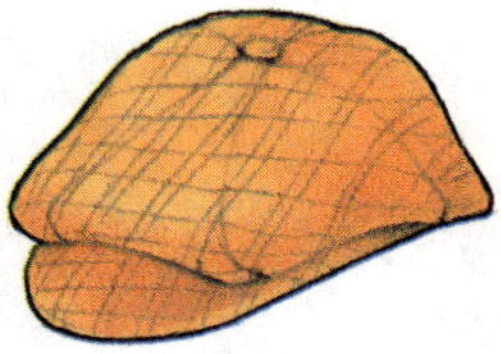

cap	b_t
h_t	v_n
l_mp	fl_g

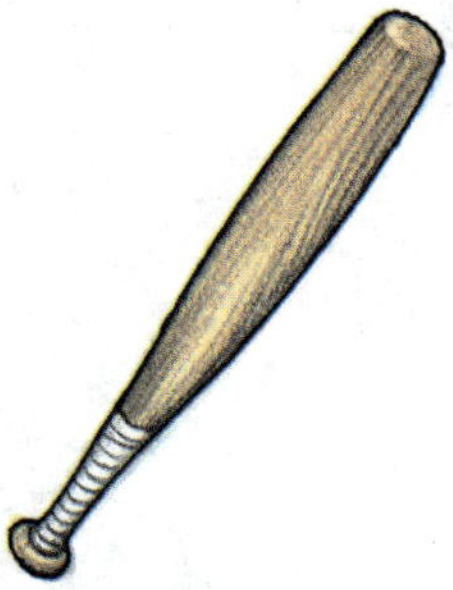

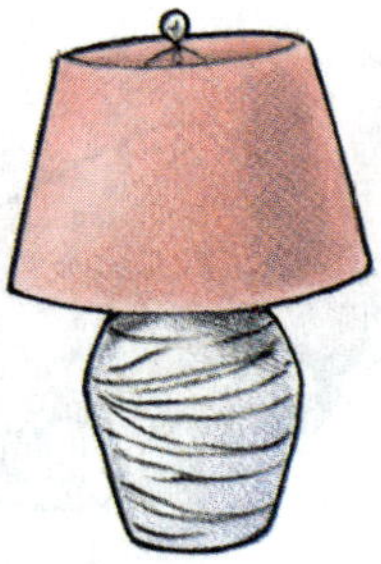

Lesson 11 49

12 Fox and Box

Ring the pictures with the same middle sound as

fox

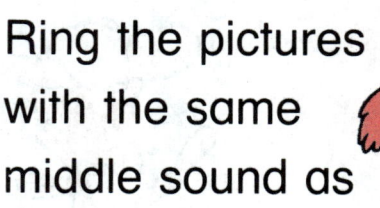

50   Lesson 12

Match the middle sounds.

Lesson 12

Name the picture.
Listen for the short *o* sound.
Write the letter *o*.

52 Lesson 12

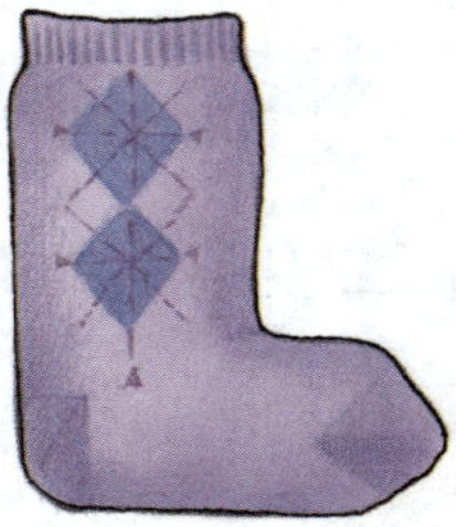

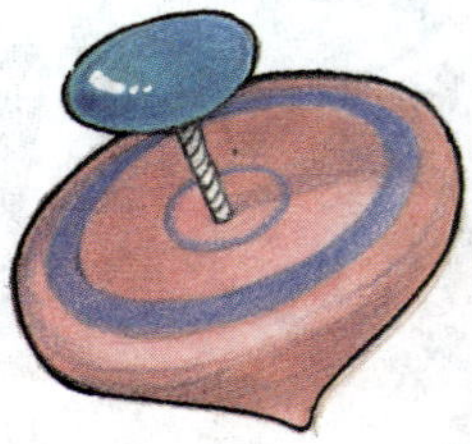

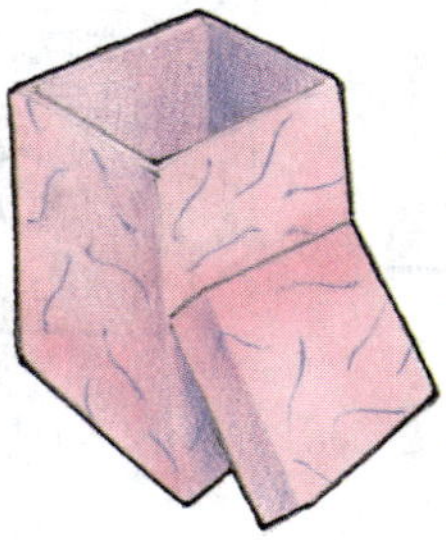

Name the picture.
Write the letter.

pot

r o ck

f o x

m o p

d o ll

l o ck

Lesson 12

13
My Trunk on the Truck

Ring the pictures with the same middle sound as  duck

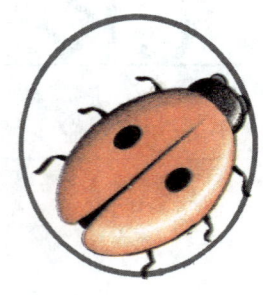

Match the middle sounds.

Lesson 13

Name the picture.
Listen for the short *u* sound.
Write the letter *u*.

duck (u)	tub	sun
fox	bug	lamp
drum	bus	belt
brush	6	skunk

56 Lesson 13

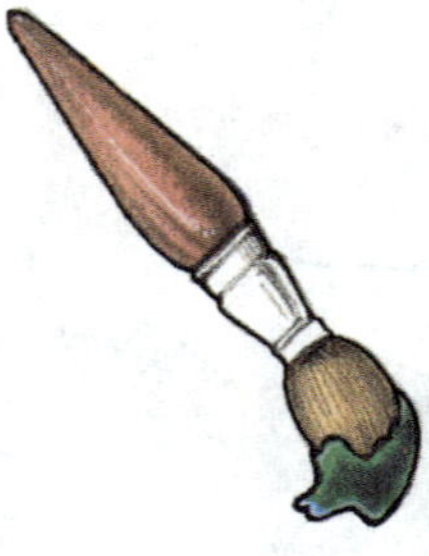

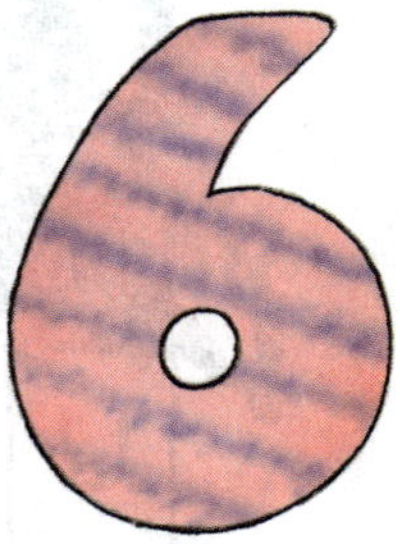

Name the picture.
Write the letter.

sun

b_s

dr_m

c_p

tr_ck

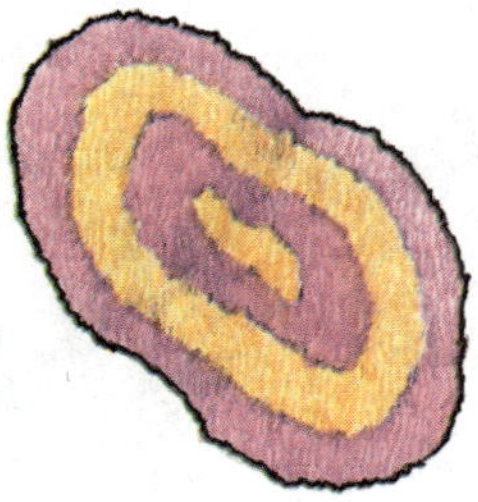

r_g

14
My Desk at School

Ring the pictures with the same middle sound as  hen

  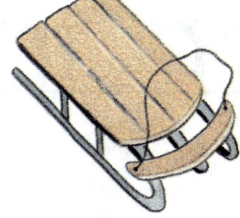 

58   Lesson 14

Match the middle sounds.

Lesson 14

Name the picture.
Listen for the short *e* sound.
Write the letter *e*.

desk — e	belt —	(ten) —
sun —	vest —	bell —
six —	bag —	shell —
bed —	van —	tent —

60   Lesson 14

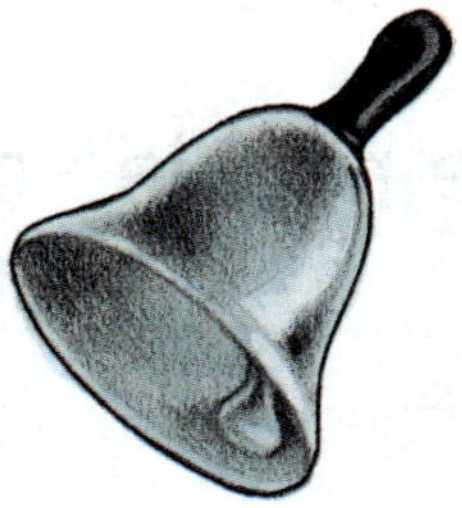

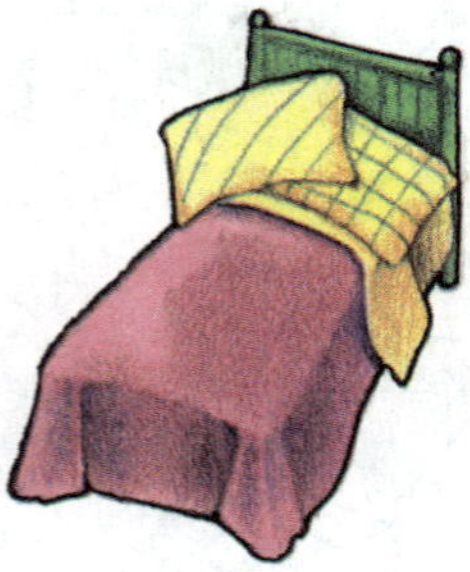

Name the picture.
Write the letter.

n_et	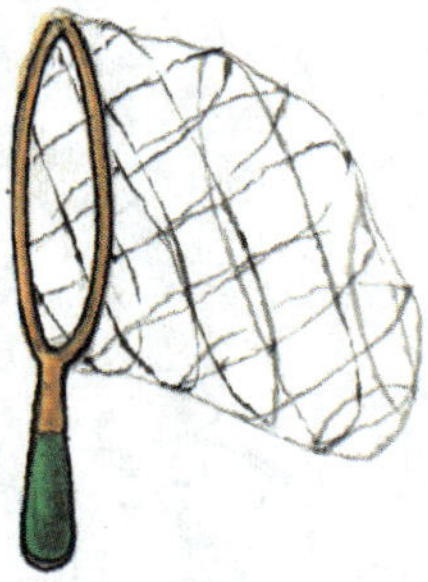  b_d
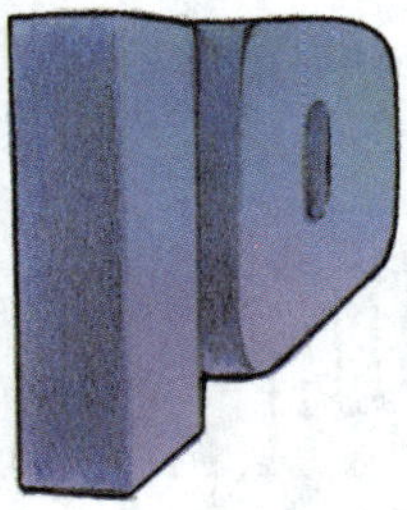 t_n	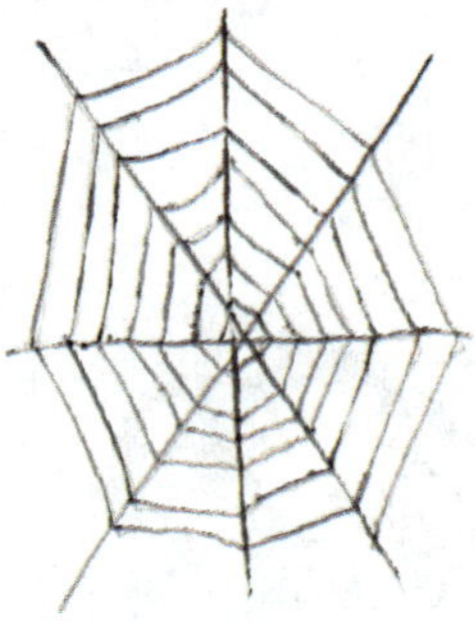 w_b
 v_st	 s_d

Lesson 14 61

15 What's for Dinner?

Ring the pictures with the same middle sound as
pig

 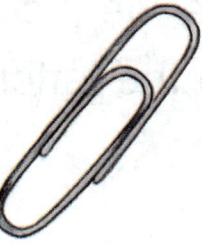

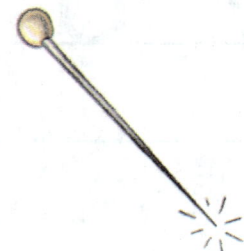   

Lesson 15

Match the middle sounds.

Lesson 15

Name the picture.
Listen for the short *i* sound.
Write the letter *i*.

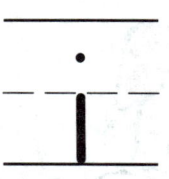

64 Lesson 15

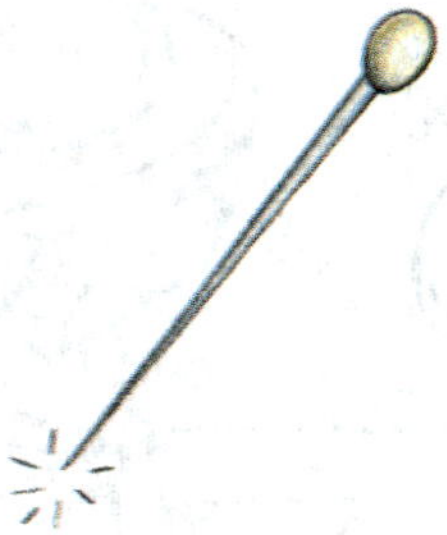

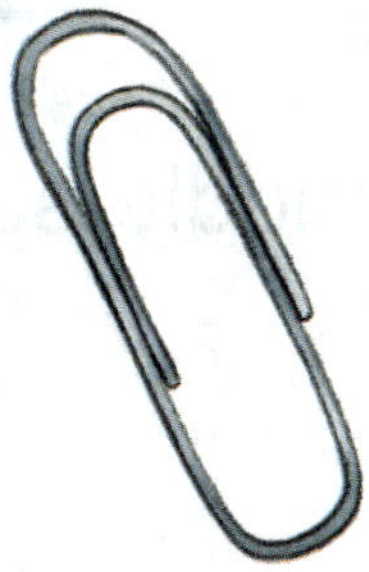

Name the picture.
Write the letter.

b i b

s i x

p i n

h i l l

f i sh

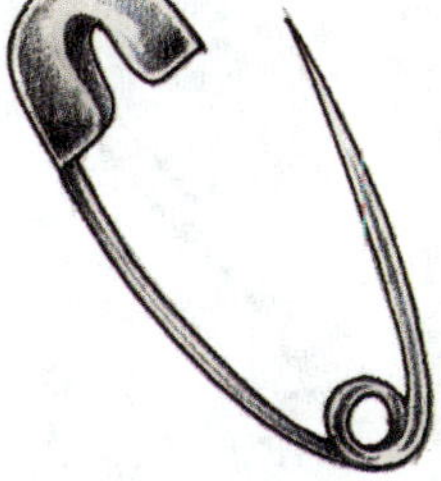

br i ck

Lesson 15

16
A Wonderful Pet

Match the middle sounds.

Name the picture.
Listen for the middle sound.
Ring the letter.

Lesson 16

Name the picture.
Listen for the middle sound.
Write the letter.

a e i o u

68   Lesson 16

Name the picture.
Write the letter.

a e i o u

Lesson 16

17 Dad Ran

CORE

FOCUS

1. dad dad
2. ran
3. can
4. cat
5. sat
6. bag

Say *dad* and *ran*.

Listen for the middle sound.

It is called the short *a* sound.

Write *dad* and *ran*. Ring the letter that spells the short *a* sound.

Now do the same with the other words.

CHALLENGE

7. fan   8. had   9. am   10. and

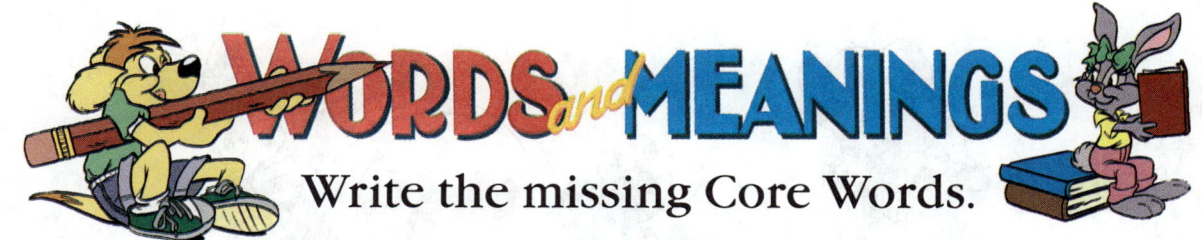

Words and Meanings

Write the missing Core Words.

A Fast Cat

_____ _____

The _____ jumped out of the _____ .

_____ _____

My _____ and I _____ after the cat.

_____

At last we _____ down on the grass.

_____

That cat _____ run fast.

Word Works

- Add the letters *an* to make words.

The m_____ sat in the v_____ .

- Add the letters *at* to make words.

He had a baseball b_____ and a h_____ .

Lesson 17

A. Name the pictures.

B. Write the Core Words that rhyme with the picture names.

CHALLENGE WORDS

C. Write the Challenge Words where they belong. Ring the letter that spells short *a* in each word.

I _____ hot _____ tired.

I wish I _____ a _____ .

Lesson 17

Write about a race you saw
or a race you ran in.
Spell the words as well as you can.

PROOFREADING PRACTICE

Cross out the six mistakes.
Write the right words on the lines.

My dod runs. He kan run fast. He run in the park. Then he sot down. He opened the bog. A small kat jumped out.

_____   _____   _____

_____   _____   _____

Now proofread your writing.

CORE		CHALLENGE	
dad	cat	fan	am
ran	sat	had	and
can	bag		

Lesson 17   73

18 Hop on Top

CORE

1. top   top
2. box
3. hop
4. fox
5. hot
6. not

> Say *top* and *box*.
>
> Listen for the middle sound.
>
> It is called the short *o* sound.
>
> Write *top* and *box*. Ring the letter that spells the short *o* sound.
>
> Now do the same with the other words.

CHALLENGE

7. mom   8. pop   9. got   10. pot

Write the missing Core Words.

Fox on a Box

Look at the _____ .

It is on _____ of the _____ .

Can you _____ up there, too?

I can _____ do it. I am too _____ !

- Add the letters *ot* to make words. Ring the word that names the picture.

l ____   c ____   sp ____

- Add the letters *op* to make words. Ring the word that names the picture.

m ____   sh ____

Lesson 18   75

A. Name each picture. Write the Core Word or Words that have the same beginning sound as each picture name.

_____   _____

_____   _____   _____

CHALLENGE WORDS

B. Write the Challenge Words that begin and end the same.

_____   _____

Here are my _____ and _____.

C. Write the Challenge Words that rhyme.

_____   _____

They have _____ a _____.

76   Lesson 18

WRITE ON YOUR OWN

Do you like to hop?
Write about what you do.
Spell the words as well as you can.

DICTIONARY WORKOUT

a b c d e f g h i j k l m n o p q r s t u v w x y z

Trace the letters.
Write the missing letters.

a b ___ d
m ___ o p ___ r
u ___ w ___ y z

Now proofread your writing.

CORE		CHALLENGE	
top	fox	mom	got
box	not	pop	pot
hop	hot		

Lesson 18 77

19 Run in the Sun

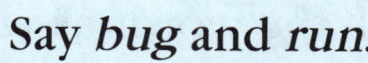

CORE

1. bug   bug
2. run
3. but
4. sun
5. nut
6. hug

Say *bug* and *run*.

Listen for the middle sound.

It is called the short *u* sound.

Write *bug* and *run*. Ring the letter that spells the short *u* sound.

Now do the same with the other words.

CHALLENGE

7. bus   8. cup   9. fun   10. tub

Words and Meanings

Write the missing Core Words.

My Pup

My pup and I _____ in the _____ .

My pup finds a _____ , _____ it runs away. We sit under a _____ tree.

I give my pup a _____ .

• Add the letters *ug* to make words.

j_____   m_____   r_____

• Add the letters *ut* to make words.

n_____   c_____   sh_____

Lesson 19   79

A. Read each clue. Listen for short *u*. Write two Core Words that rhyme with the words below. Ring the Core Word that names the picture.

cut _____ _____

rug _____ _____

bun _____ _____

CHALLENGE WORDS

B. Write the Challenge Word that fits the clue.

Wash in it. _____

Drink from it. _____

Ride in it. _____

Have a good time. _____

80   Lesson 19

 WRITE ON YOUR OWN

What do you like to do in the sun?
Write about it.
Spell the words as well as you can.

PROOFREADING PRACTICE

The first word in a sentence begins with a capital letter. Write the sentence correctly. Use a capital letter.

see the bug run.

_____

- - - - - - - - - - - - - - - - - - - -

_____

Now proofread your writing.

CORE		CHALLENGE	
bug	sun	bus	fun
run	nut	cup	tub
but	hug		

Lesson 19 81

20 A Pet Hen

CORE

1. pet   pet
2. hen
3. get
4. net
5. wet
6. leg

> Say *pet* and *hen*.
>
> Listen for the middle sound.
>
> It is called the short *e* sound.
>
> Write *pet* and *hen*. Ring the letter that spells the short *e* sound.
>
> Now do the same with the other words.

CHALLENGE

7. beg   8. jet   9. web   10. yes

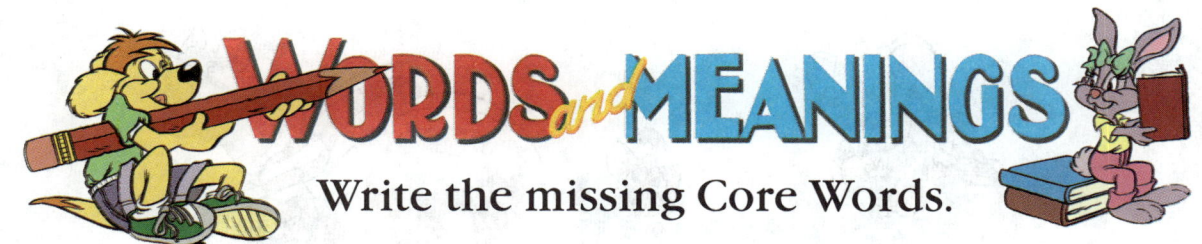

Write the missing Core Words.

A Wet Hen

_____ _____

How did you _____ so _____?

_____ _____

My _____ _____ ran out in the rain.

_____ _____

Her _____ was stuck in a _____.

Word Works

• Add the letters *en* to make words.

T____ m____

d____

sat in a lion's d____.

• Add the letters *et* to make words.

m____ y____

I have not m____ them y____.

Lesson 20

A. Name the pictures.
Write the Core Word that has the same beginning sound as each picture name.
Use *e* to spell the short *e* sound.

CHALLENGE WORDS

B. Write the Challenge Word that goes with each clue.

a spider's home

ask

a plane

not no

84   Lesson 20

Think of a pet you would like to have. Write about it. Spell the words as well as you can.

DICTIONARY WORKOUT

Words in a dictionary are in ABC order.

a b c d e f g h i j k l m n o p q r s t u v w x y z

Write the missing letters below.

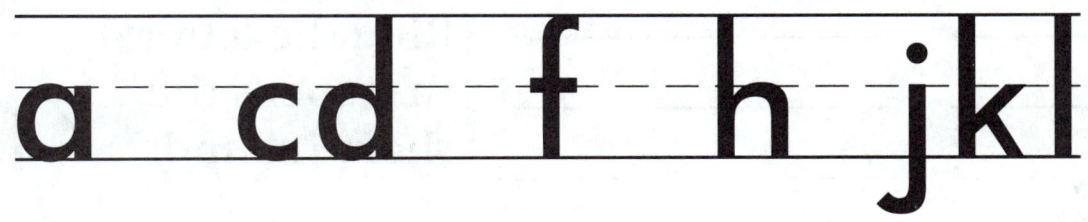

a ___ c d ___ f ___ h ___ j k l

m ___ o ___ q ___ s ___ u v ___ x ___ z

Now proofread your writing.

CORE		CHALLENGE	
pet	net	beg	web
hen	wet	jet	yes
get	leg		

Lesson 20   **85**

21 Did Pig Win?

CORE

1. pig   pig
2. win
3. did
4. big
5. in
6. sit

> Say *pig* and *win*.
>
> Listen for the middle sound.
>
> It is called the short *i* sound.
>
> Write *pig* and *win*. Ring the letter that spells the short *i* sound.
>
> Now do the same with the other words.

CHALLENGE

7. dig   8. fin   9. him   10. is

WORDS and MEANINGS

Write the missing Core Words.

A First Prize Hat

My pet _____ won first prize _____ a show. What _____ she _____? She won a _____ hat. I hope she does not _____ on it!

WORDworks

• Add the letters *it* to make words.

f_____   h_____   l_____

• Add the letters *id* to make words.
  Ring the word that names the picture.

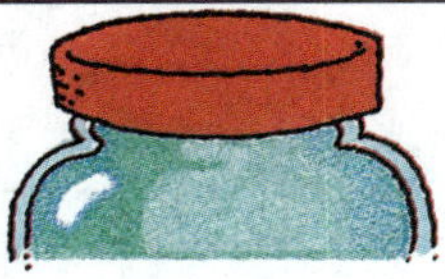

k_____   h_____   l_____

Lesson 21   87

A. Name each picture. Write the Core Words that rhyme with each picture name.

B. Name each picture. Write the Core Word that has the same beginning sound as each picture name.

CHALLENGE WORDS

C. Put the letters in order to spell Challenge Words. Write the Challenge Words.

i n f _____

g i d _____

s i _____

i m h _____

88   Lesson 21

WRITE ON YOUR OWN

What does a pig look like?
What does a pig do?
Write about pigs.
Spell the words as well as you can.

PROOFREADING PRACTICE

A sentence that asks a question ends with a question mark. Write the sentence correctly. Use a question mark.

Did the pig win.

D _____

Now proofread your writing.

CORE		CHALLENGE	
pig	big	dig	him
win	in	fin	is
did	sit		

Lesson 21   89

22 Club Flip Flop

CORE

1. clam   clam
2. flip
3. clap
4. flag
5. club
6. flat

> Say *clam* and *flip*.
>
> Listen to the first two sounds.
>
> Write *clam* and *flip*. Ring the two letters in each word that spell the first two sounds.
>
> Now do the same with the other words.

CHALLENGE

7. class   8. clip   9. flap   10. fly

Lesson 22

Words and Meanings

Write the Core Words that go with the pictures.

- Add the letters *at* to make words. Ring the word that names the picture.

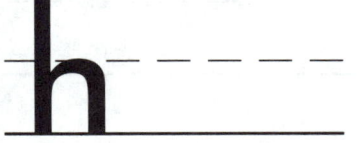 m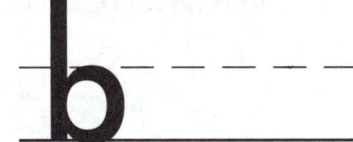

- Add the letters *ap* to make words. Ring the word that names the picture.

l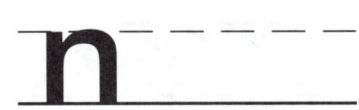

Lesson 22   91

A. Name the picture. Write the Core Words that have the same beginning sound as the picture name.

_____   _____   _____

_____   _____   _____

B. Write the Core Words that begin with *cl*.

_____   _____   _____

_____   _____   _____

CHALLENGE WORDS

C. Write the Challenge Word that fits each clue. Ring that letters that spell the two beginning sounds.

rhymes with *glass*

_____

what birds and jets do

_____

to cut off the ends

_____

the door of a tent

_____

92   Lesson 22

WRITE ON YOUR OWN

Make up a club for you and your friends.
Write about your club.
Spell the words as well as you can.

DICTIONARY WORKOUT

Words in a dictionary are in ABC order.

a b c d e f g h i j k l m n o p q r s t u v w x y z

Write the words below in ABC order.

boys   dig   can   all

1. _____   3. _____

2. _____   4. _____

Now proofread your writing.

CORE		CHALLENGE	
clam	flag	class	flap
flip	club	clip	fly
clap	flat		

Lesson 22

23 You Are You

FOCUS

CORE

1. are   are
2. said
3. all
4. I
5. you
6. the

Say *are* and *said*.

Look at how each word is spelled. These words are not spelled the way they sound. You must remember the spelling.

Write the words. Remember the spelling.

CHALLENGE

7. here   8. love   9. of   10. was

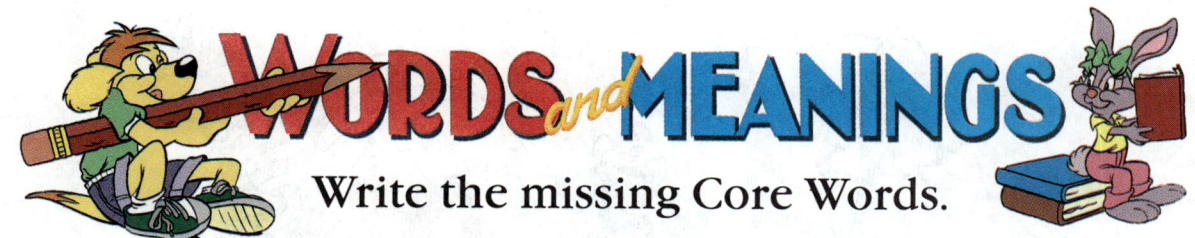

Write the missing Core Words.

A Zoo Trip

Our class went to _____ zoo.

"I am glad to see _____," _____ the man. "Where _____ you going?"

"We are going _____ over the zoo," we said.

- Add *s* to make words that mean more than one.

hat   hats

cat   mop   pig

leg   bug   pet

Lesson 23   95

A. Name each picture. Write the Core Words that rhyme with the picture names.

_____ _____ _____

B. Write the Core Words that sound like the names of these letters.

_____   _____

i _____   r _____

C. Write the Core Word that begins with the letters *th*.

_____

CHALLENGE WORDS

D. Find the letters that spell the Challenge Words. Ring the letters. Write the Challenge Words.

mnofvcyt _____

dxlovefg _____   bacqhere _____   waszptho _____

96   Lesson 23

WRITE ON YOUR OWN

Who are you? Tell about yourself. Spell the words as well as you can.

I LIKE TO SWIM
I HAVE STRONG TEETH

PROOFREADING PRACTICE

Cross out the five mistakes. Write the right words on the lines.

"Look at oll tha flags," sed Dick. "Can yu name them?" asked Ann. "There ar too many," I said.

_____   _____   _____

_____   _____

_____

Now proofread your writing.

CORE		CHALLENGE	
are	I	here	of
said	you	love	was
all	the		

Lesson 23   97

24 REVIEW

LESSON 17   Read the Core Words. Name each picture. Write the Core Word that has the same ending sound as each picture name.

bag
can
dad
sat

_____ _____

_____ _____

FOCUS   Ring the letter that spells the short *a* sound in each word.

LESSON 18   Read the Core Words. Name each picture. Write the Core Word that has the same beginning sound as each picture name.

fox
hot
top
box

_____ _____

_____ _____

FOCUS   Ring the letter that spells the short *o* sound in each word.

REVIEW

LESSON 19 Read the Core Words. Name each picture. Write the Core Word or Words that have the same ending sound as each picture name.

but
bug
run
nut

FOCUS Ring the letter that spells the short *u* sound in each word.

LESSON 20 Read the Core Words. Name each picture. Write the Core Word or Words that rhyme with each picture name.

get
hen
leg
wet

FOCUS Ring the letter that spells the short *e* sound in each word.

Lesson 24   99

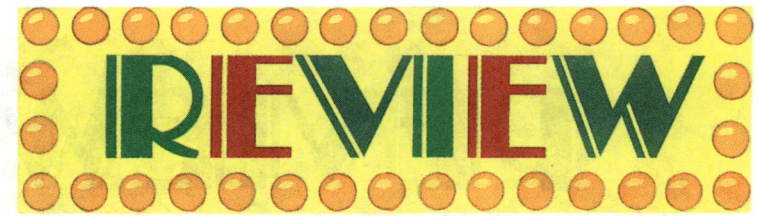

LESSON 21 Read the Core Words. Name each picture. Write the Core Word that has the same beginning sound as each picture name.

big
did
sit
win

FOCUS Ring the letter that spells the short *i* sound in each word.

LESSON 22 Read the Core Words. Name each picture. Write the Core Word that rhymes with each picture name.

flag
club
flat
clap

FOCUS Ring the two letters that spell the beginning sounds in each word.

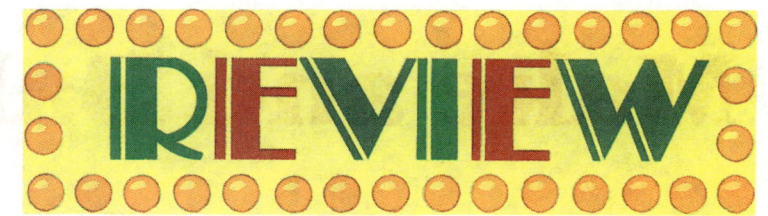

LESSON 23   Read the Core Words. Name each picture. Write the Core Word that rhymes with each picture name.

all
are
I
said

FOCUS   Ring the two words that are the hardest for you to spell.

- Add the letters *ap* to make words. Ring the word that names the picture.

c   **n**   **m**

- Add the letters *ip* to make words. Ring the word that names the picture.

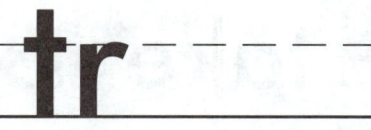

z   **dr**   **tr**

Lesson 24   101

25 Make and Bake

CORE

1. made made
2. bake
3. name
4. game
5. gave
6. ate

> Say *made* and *bake*.
>
> Listen for the middle sound.
>
> It is called the long *a* sound. The letters *a* and *e* can spell the long *a* sound.
>
> Write *made* and *bake*. Ring the letters that spell the long *a* sound.
>
> Now do the same with the other words.

CHALLENGE

7. take 8. came 9. same 10. gate

Lesson 25

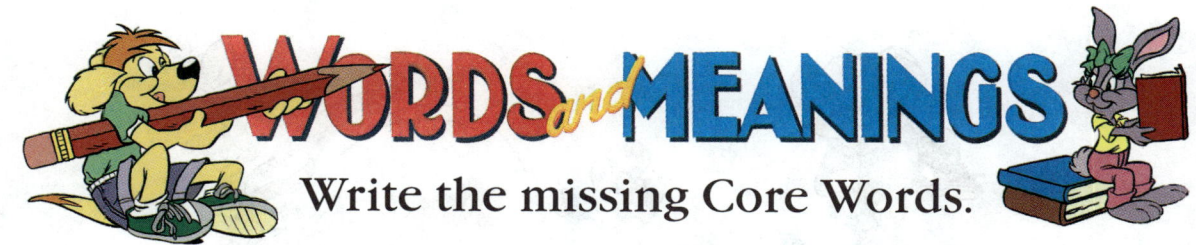

Write the missing Core Words.

Baking Bread

My uncle's _____ is Dave. He likes to _____ bread. We _____ some. Uncle Dave mixed. Then he _____ me a turn. It was like a _____. We _____ the bread.

- Add the letters *ake* to make words.

I saw a sn____ by the l____. I began to sh____.

- Add the letters *ave* to make words.

I was not br____. I hid in a c____.

Lesson 25

A. Name each picture.
Write the Core Word or Words that have the same beginning sound as each picture name.

CHALLENGE WORDS

B. Read the words below. Write the Challenge Words that rhyme with them.

ate _____   bake _____

game _____

Think of a fun thing you would like to make. Write about it. Spell the words as well as you can.

DICTIONARY WORKOUT

Words in a dictionary are in ABC order.

a b c d e f g h i j k l m n o p q r s t u v w x y z

Write the letter that comes after each letter below.

c _____   i _____   n _____

t _____   x _____

Write the letter that comes before each letter below.

_____ c   _____ h   _____ i   _____ q   _____ x

Now proofread your writing.

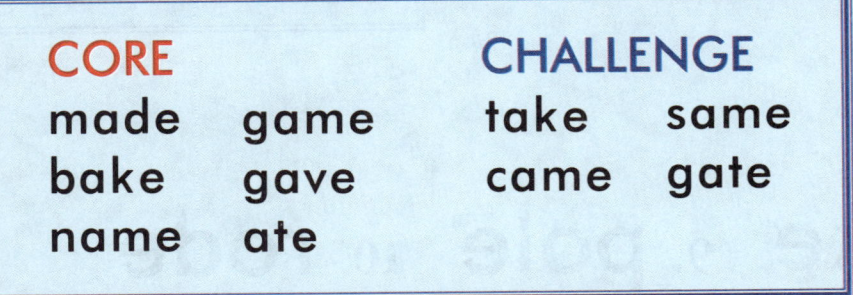

CORE		CHALLENGE	
made	game	take	same
bake	gave	came	gate
name	ate		

Lesson 25   **105**

26 Notes on Bone

CORE

1. go   go
2. note
3. no
4. home
5. bone
6. rope

> Say *go* and *note*.
>
> Listen for the last sound in *go*. Listen for the middle sound in *note*. It is called the long *o* sound.
>
> The long *o* sound may be spelled *o* or *o* and *e*.
>
> Write *go* and *note*. Ring the letters that spell the long *o* sound.
>
> Now do the same with the other words.

CHALLENGE

7. hope   8. joke   9. pole   10. rode

Words and Meanings

Write the missing Core Words.

Visiting Pat

_____ I tied a _____ to the wagon. Rover put

his _____ in the wagon. We will _____

to see Pat. Then I will take Rover _____ .

- Read the clues. Write the Core Words that match them.

not yes _____   a little letter _____

Word Works

- Add the letter *s* to make words that mean more than one.

home   bone   rope

game   note   name

Lesson 26   107

A. Write the Core Word that rhymes with each picture name.

B. Write the Core Word that has the same beginning sound as each picture name. Use words with long *o* spelled *o*.

CHALLENGE WORDS

C. Write the Challenge Word that begins like each picture name.

Lesson 26

Think about a time in the past. What was it like? Write about this time. Spell the words as well as you can.

PROOFREADING PRACTICE

Cross out three spelling mistakes. Write the right words on the lines.

I came hom from school.
Rover wanted to gow for a walk.
He wanted to find his bon.

_____   _____   _____

Now proofread your writing.

CORE		CHALLENGE	
go	home	hope	pole
note	bone	joke	rode
no	rope		

Lesson 26   **109**

27 See Me Weed

CORE

1. me   me
2. weed
3. he
4. seed
5. bee
6. see

> Say *me* and *weed*.
>
> Listen for the last sound in *me*. Listen for the middle sound in *weed*. It is called the long *e* sound.
>
> The long *e* sound may be spelled *e* or *ee*.
>
> Write *me* and *weed*. Ring the letters that spell the long *e* sound.
>
> Now do the same with the other words.

CHALLENGE

7. she   8. feel   9. feet   10. jeep

Words and Meanings

Write the missing Core Words.

A Bee Sting

Dad gave _____ an apple _____.

Then _____ pulled up a _____. But

he did not _____ the _____. Ouch!

- Add the letters *eed* to make words.

d___ n___ f___

- Add the letters *eep* to make words.

d___ k___ w___

- Ring the word that names the picture.

Lesson 27   111

A. The long *e* sound can be spelled *e*. Write the Core Word that has the same beginning sound as each picture name.

B. The long *e* sound can be spelled *ee*. Write the Core Word or Words that have the same beginning sound as each picture name.

CHALLENGE WORDS

C. Ring the four words that do not belong. Then write the Challenge Words that rhyme with them.

Did tree miss the sheep?
Her beet will peel very hot.

What kind of garden would you like?
Write about it.
Spell the words as well as you can.

DICTIONARY WORKOUT

Words in a dictionary are in ABC order.

a b c d e f g h i j k l m n o p q r s t u v w x y z

Write the words in ABC order.

see   feet   he   bee   weed   me

1. _____   3. _____   5. _____

2. _____   4. _____   6. _____

Now proofread your writing.

CORE		CHALLENGE	
me	seed	she	feet
weed	bee	feel	jeep
he	see		

Lesson 27   113

28 Bike Ride Time

CORE

1. bike   bike
2. ride
3. like
4. kite
5. time
6. hide

> Say *bike* and *ride*.
>
> Listen for the middle sound. It is called the long *i* sound.
>
> The letters *i* and *e* can spell the long *i* sound.
>
> Write *bike* and *ride*. Ring the letters that spell the long *i* sound.
>
> Now do the same with the other words.

CHALLENGE

7. fine   8. mine   9. dime   10. size

Words and Meanings

Write the missing Core Words.

At the Park

I _____ to _____ my _____ in the park. Sometimes I _____ it behind a bush. Then I fly my _____. I have a good _____.

• Add the letters *ide* to make words.

The t_____ is out. The beach is w_____. The sea gulls gl_____ in the air.

• Add the letters *ite* to make words.

The sand is wh_____. I got a b_____!

Lesson 28   115

A. Write the Core Word that has the same beginning sound as each picture name.

CHALLENGE WORDS

B. Put the letters in order to make Challenge Words. Ring the letters that spell long *i*.

nfie _____   ezis _____

enmi _____   idme _____

116   Lesson 28

Think about a bike ride you would like to take. Write about it. Spell the words as well as you can.

DICTIONARY WORKOUT

Words in a dictionary are in ABC order.

a b c d e f g h i j k l m n o p q r s t u v w x y z

Write the Core Words in ABC order.

hide   ride   bike   like   time   kite

1. _____   3. _____   5. _____

2. _____   4. _____   6. _____

Now proofread your writing.

CORE		CHALLENGE	
bike	kite	fine	dime
ride	time	mine	size
like	hide		

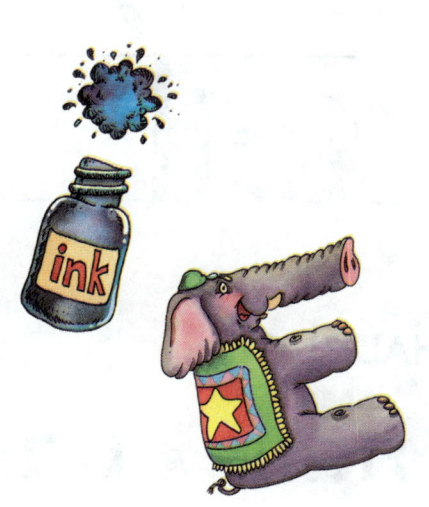

Lesson 28

29 Day of Rain

CORE

1. day day
2. rain
3. may
4. wait
5. way
6. tail

> Say *day* and *rain*.
>
> Listen for the long *a* sound.
>
> In these words the long *a* sound is spelled *ay* or *ai*.
>
> Write *day* and *rain*. Ring the letters that spell the long *a* sound.
>
> Now do the same with the other words.

CHALLENGE

7. nail 8. paint 9. clay 10. play

118   Lesson 29

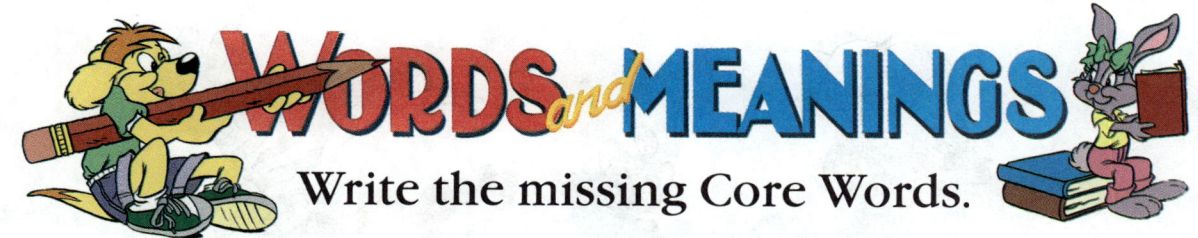

A Rainy Day

The _____ came down all night.

There is no _____ to stop it. Toby wags

his _____ . He can't _____ to play.

But we _____ have to stay in all _____ .

- Add the letters *ay* to make words.

What do you p_____ for h_____?

- Add the letters *ail* to make words.

How do you s_____ in a p_____?

Lesson 29

A. The long *a* sound can be spelled *ai*. Write the Core Word that rhymes with each picture name.

_____   _____   _____

B. The long *a* sound can be spell *ay*. Write the Core Word that has the same beginning sound as each picture name.

_____   _____   _____

CHALLENGE WORDS

C. Write the Challenge Words that fit each clue. Ring the letters that spell the long *a* sound in each word.

hammer _____   _____
and   _____   work and _____

                       _____
brush and _____   dirt and _____

120   Lesson 29

What are some nice things about rain?
Write about them.
Check for capitals and periods.

PROOFREADING PRACTICE

A sentence begins with a capital letter.
A telling sentence ends with a period.
Write these sentences correctly.

it may rain all day
there is a way to play

_____

_____

_____

_____

Now proofread your writing.

CORE		CHALLENGE	
day	wait	nail	clay
rain	way	paint	play
may	tail		

Lesson 29

30 REVIEW

LESSON 25 Read the Core Words. Name each picture. Write the Core Word that rhymes with each picture name.

bake
game
ate
gave

FOCUS Ring the two letters that spell the long *a* sound in each word.

LESSON 26 Read the Core Words. Name each picture. Write the Core Word that has the same beginning sound as each picture name.

go
no
bone
rope

FOCUS Ring the letter or letters that spell the long *o* sound in each word.

LESSON 27 — Read the Core Words. Name each picture. Write the Core Word that has the same beginning sound as each picture name.

he
me
see
weed

_____   _____
_____   _____
_____   _____
_____   _____

FOCUS Ring the letter or letters that spell the long *e* sound in each word.

LESSON 28 — Read the Core Words. Name each picture. Write the Core Word that has the same beginning sound as each picture name.

bike
kite
ride
time

_____   _____
_____   _____
_____   _____
_____   _____

FOCUS Ring the two letters that spell the long *i* sound in each word.

Lesson 30   **123**

LESSON 29   Read the Core Words. Name each picture. Write the word that rhymes with each picture name.

day
rain
wait
tail

 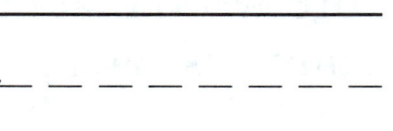 

FOCUS   Ring the two letters that spell the long *a* sound in each word.

- Add the letters *ate* to make words. Ring the word that names the picture.

sk_____   d_____   st_____

- Add the letters *eed* to make words. Ring the word that names the picture.

n_____   s_____   f_____

124   Lesson 30

REVIEW

DICTIONARY WORKOUT

Remember that words in a dictionary are in ABC order.

a b c d e f g h i j k l m n o p q r s t u v w x y z

Write the Core Words in ABC order.

kite   like   ate   me   no   bone

1. _____   3. _____   5. _____

2. _____   4. _____   6. _____

PROOFREADING PRACTICE

Cross out the three spelling mistakes. Write the right words on the lines.

My nam is Stan.
I carry my hom on my back.
It keeps the rane away.

_____   _____   _____

Lesson 30

31 Stop for the Snake

CORE

1. stop   stop
2. snake
3. snail
4. snap
5. step
6. stay

FOCUS

Say *stop* and *snake*.

Listen for the first two sounds.

Write *stop* and *snake*. Ring the letters that spell the first two sounds in each word.

Now do the same with the other words.

CHALLENGE

7. snug   8. snore   9. stone   10. stove

Words and Meanings

Write the missing Core Word.

A Snake on the Path

Ron heard a twig _____. He did not _____ running. He was not slow like a _____. He had to _____ over a _____ on the path. He did not _____ on the path.

Word Works

- Add the letters *ug* to make words.

  I will help you t_____

  the r_____. Then you give me a h_____.

- Add the letters *ay* to make words.

  Now m_____ I go out to pl_____?

Lesson 31   127

A. Name each picture. Write the Core Words that have the same beginning sounds as each picture name.

_____ _____ _____

_____ _____ _____

CHALLENGE WORDS

B. Write two Challenge Words that have the same beginning sounds as *stay* and *stop*.

_____ _____

C. Write two Challenge Words that have the same beginning sounds as *snake* and *snail*.

_____ _____

Think of some good things about snakes. Write about them. Spell the words as well as you can.

DICTIONARY WORKOUT

Words in a dictionary are in ABC order.
Many words begin with the same letter.
The second letter helps you put them in order.

a b c d e f g h i j k l m n o p q r s t u v w x y z

Write the words in ABC order.

step   sun   said   snail   send   sock

1. _____
2. _____
3. _____
4. _____
5. _____
6. _____

Now proofread your writing.

CORE		CHALLENGE	
stop	snap	snug	stone
snake	step	snore	stove
snail	stay		

Lesson 31   129

32 This Chat

CORE

1. this   this
2. chat
3. chop
4. that
5. then
6. chin

> Say *this* and *chat*.
>
> Listen for the first sound in each word.
>
> Write *this* and *chat*. Ring the two letters that spell the first sound in each word.
>
> Now do the same with the other words.

CHALLENGE

7. chain   8. chase   9. these   10. those

Words and Meanings

Write the Core Word that fits each clue.

small talk _____   something over there _____

in the past _____   part of your jaw _____

something here _____   cut into small parts _____

- Add the letters *en* to make words.

m____   h____   th____

- Add the letters *in* to make words.

p____   w____   ch____

- Ring the words that name the pictures.

A. Name each picture. Write the Core Word that ends with the same sound. Use the Core Words that begin with *ch*.

B. Write the Core Words that end with the same sound as each picture name. Use Core Words that begin with *th*.

CHALLENGE WORDS

C. Write the Challenge Words that begin the same as *then*.

D. Write the Challenge Words that begin the same as the picture name.

What did people do long ago?
How did they go from place to place?
Write about what you think it was like.
Spell the words as well as you can.

PROOFREADING PRACTICE

Cross out the four spelling mistakes.
Write the right Core Words on the lines.

Grandpa and I had a long chot. He said, "I planted thaat tree over there. I was only a boy than. Will you help me plant thiss new one?"

_____   _____

_____   _____

_____   _____

_____   _____

Now proofread your writing.

CORE		CHALLENGE	
this	that	chain	these
chat	then	chase	those
chop	chin		

Lesson 32

33 Which Ship

CORE

1. which   which
2. ship
3. shop
4. whale
5. when
6. shape

Say *which* and *ship*.

Listen for the first sound in each word.

Write *which* and *ship*. Ring the two letters that spell the first sound in each word.

Now do the same with the other words.

CHALLENGE

7. shark   8. shell   9. where   10. why

Words and Meanings

Write the missing Core Words.

The Toy Shop

_____

The toy _____ is on my street. A bell rings _____ you go in. There is a sailing _____ . There is a gray _____ .

I like the _____ of it. Do you know _____ one it is?

Word Works

- Add the letters *ip* to make words. Ring the word that names the picture.

cl____   sk____

Lesson 33   135

A. Write the Core Words that have the same beginning sound as each picture name.

CHALLENGE WORDS

B. Write the two Challenge Words that have the same beginning sound as the picture name.

C. Write the two Challenge Words that have the same beginning sound as the picture name.

Think of a place you can go on a ship.
Write about the ship and the place.
Spell the words as well as you can.

DICTIONARY WORKOUT

Words in a dictionary are in ABC order.
Many words begin with the same letter.

a b c d e f g h i j k l m n o p q r s t u v w x y z

The second letter of those words tells
the ABC order. Write these words in ABC order.

north   whale   south   shape   east   west

1. _____   3. _____   5. _____

2. _____   4. _____   6. _____

Now proofread your writing.

CORE		CHALLENGE	
which	whale	shark	where
ship	when	shell	why
shop	shape		

Lesson 33   **137**

34 They Have Come

CORE

1. they   they
2. have
3. do
4. want
5. her
6. come

> Say *they* and *have*.
>
> Look at how each word is spelled. These words are not spelled the way they sound. You must remember the spelling.
>
> Write the words. Remember the spellings.

CHALLENGE

7. for   8. from   9. some   10. my

138   Lesson 34

Words and Meanings

Write the missing Core Words.

Animal Fun

Sue ran up to _____ sister.

I _____ to see the animals.

_____ they _____ to sleep now?

When are _____ coming?

Here they _____ now!

- Add the letter *s* to make words that mean more than one.

shell   shells

bike   day   clam

Lesson 34   139

A. Name each picture. Write the Core Word that rhymes with each picture name.

B. Name each picture. Write the Core Word or Words that have the same beginning sound as each picture name.

CHALLENGE WORDS

C. Find the letters that spell the Challenge Words. Ring the letters. Write the words.

sklamys _____

affromp _____

forleng _____

issomel _____

What can you see at a circus?
Write about it.
Spell the words as well as you can.

PROOFREADING PRACTICE

Cross out the six mistakes.
Write the right Core Words on the lines.

When will the animals came? I wan to see the lions. Are thay all in cages? The elephants hav to walk in a row. The band leader spins hur baton. I can du that!

_____   _____   _____

_____   _____   _____

Now proofread your writing.

CORE		CHALLENGE	
they	want	for	some
have	her	from	my
do	come		

Lesson 34   141

35 Green Yellow Red

CORE

1. red — red
2. black
3. gray
4. green
5. white
6. yellow

Say the color words.

Listen for short and long vowel sounds. Look for spellings you have learned.

Write the words. Remember the spellings.

CHALLENGE

7. blue   8. brown   9. orange   10. purple

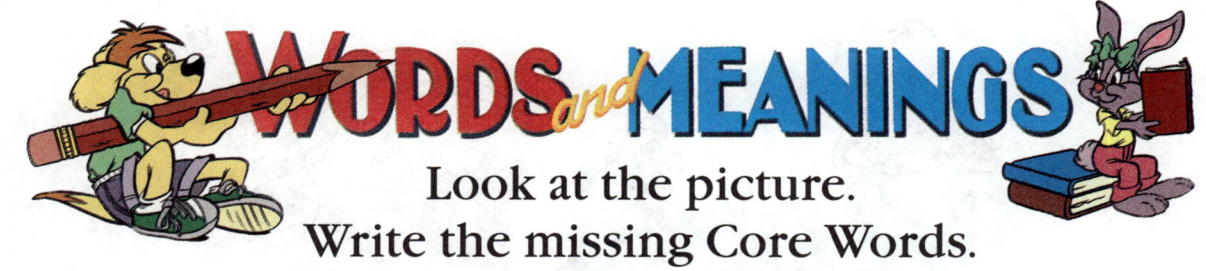

Words and Meanings

Look at the picture.
Write the missing Core Words.

Out for a Drive

A _____ car on a _____ street stopped in front of the _____ house. The driver wore a _____ hat. A big _____ ball sat on the _____ grass.

Word Works

- Add the letters *ed* to make words.
  Ring the word that names the picture.

b____   f____   sl____

Lesson 35   143

A. Name the pictures. Write the Core Word that has the same beginning sound as each picture.

CHALLENGE WORDS

B. Write the Challenge Word that goes with each group.

144   Lesson 35

WRITE ON YOUR OWN

Write about a garden filled with flowers. Use as many color words as you can. Spell the words as well as you can.

DICTIONARY WORKOUT

A dictionary tells what a word means. Write the word that goes with each meaning.

bed   name   hop   pen

a thing to write with _____

a place to sleep _____

jump up and down _____

what you call someone _____

Now proofread your writing.

CORE		CHALLENGE	
red	green	blue	orange
black	white	brown	purple
gray	yellow		

Lesson 35   145

36 REVIEW

LESSON 31   Remember *sn* in *snap* and *st* in *step*. Read the Core Words. Write the Core Word that rhymes with each picture name.

stop
snake
snail
stay

FOCUS   Ring the letters that spell the two beginning sounds in each word.

LESSON 32   Remember *ch* in *chin* and *th* in *this*. Write the Core Word or Words that rhyme with the words below.

chat
chop
that
then

pat _____   _____

men _____   pop _____

FOCUS   Ring the letters that spell the beginning sound in each word.

LESSON 33 Remember *sh* in *shop* and *wh* in *which*. Write the Core Word that rhymes with the words below.

shape
whale
when
ship

drip _____   sale _____

then _____   cape _____

FOCUS Ring the letters that spell the beginning sound in each word.

LESSON 34 Remember that some words are not spelled the way they sound. Write the Core Word that has the same beginning sound as each picture name.

come
do
have
want

FOCUS Ring the two words that are hardest for you to spell.

Lesson 36

LESSON 35 Remember color words. Name the colors. Write the color words.

red
yellow
green
black

FOCUS Ring the two color words that you like best.

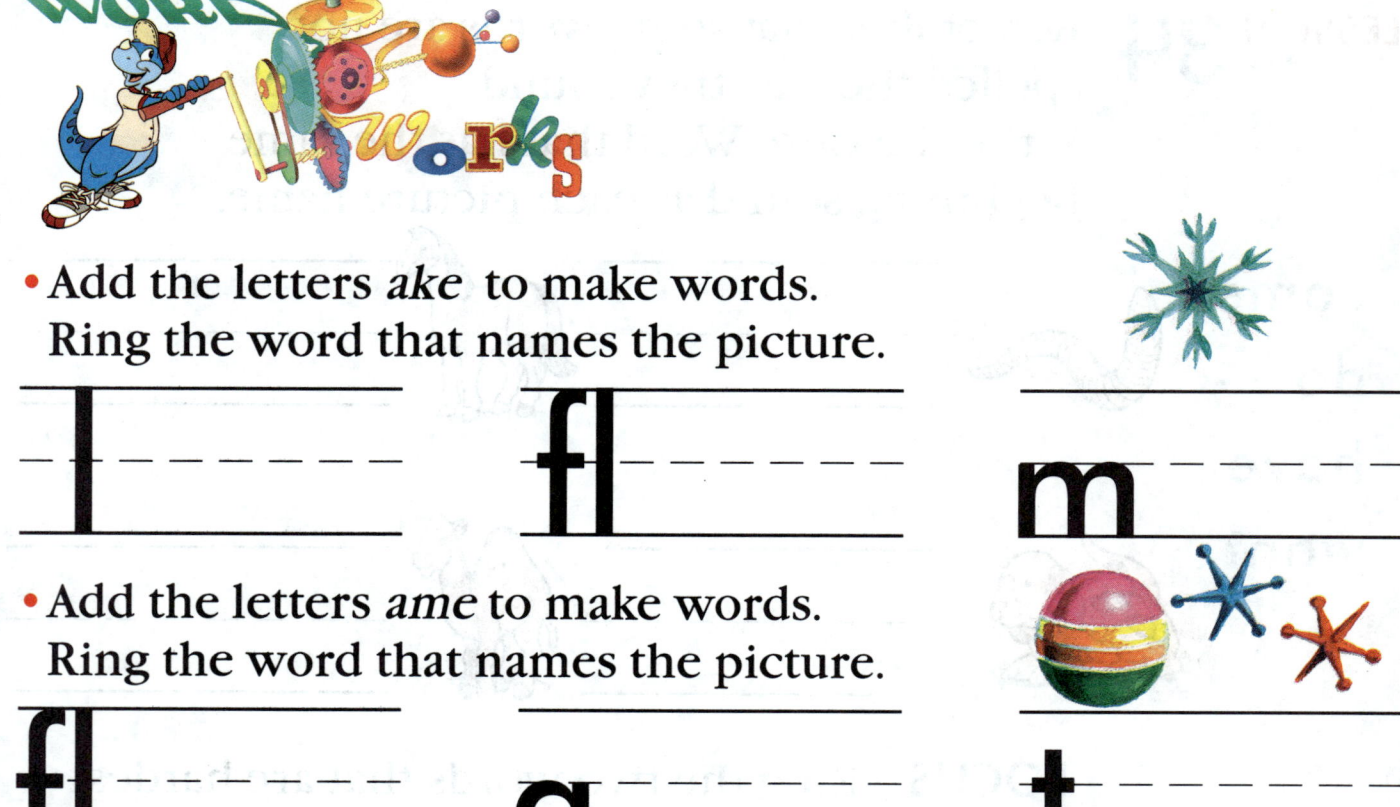

- Add the letters *ake* to make words. Ring the word that names the picture.

  l_____   fl_____   m_____

- Add the letters *ame* to make words. Ring the word that names the picture.

  fl_____   g_____   t_____

REVIEW

DICTIONARY WORKOUT

Many words in the dictionary begin with the same letter. The second letter tells the ABC order.

a b c d e f g h i j k l m n o p q r s t u v w x y z

Write the Core Words in ABC order.

snap   want   shape   stop   which   this

1. _____   3. _____   5. _____

2. _____   4. _____   6. _____

PROOFREADING PRACTICE

Remember that a telling sentence begins with a capital letter and ends with a period. Write the sentence correctly.

we saw a snake

_____

_____

Lesson 36

WHEN YOU WRITE

Read these ideas. They will help you write better stories and reports.

1. Choose an idea.
2. Think about what you will write.
3. Write your first copy.
4. Check your work.
5. Write the final copy.

PROOFREADING

Check your work. Here are some things to look for:

1. Did you start each sentence with a capital letter?
2. Did you end each sentence with the right punctuation mark?
3. Did you spell all the words correctly?

HANDWRITING

Make your writing neat and clear.
Be careful how you make the letters.
Practice your writing. Good handwriting
will help people to read what you write.
 Use these models for help.

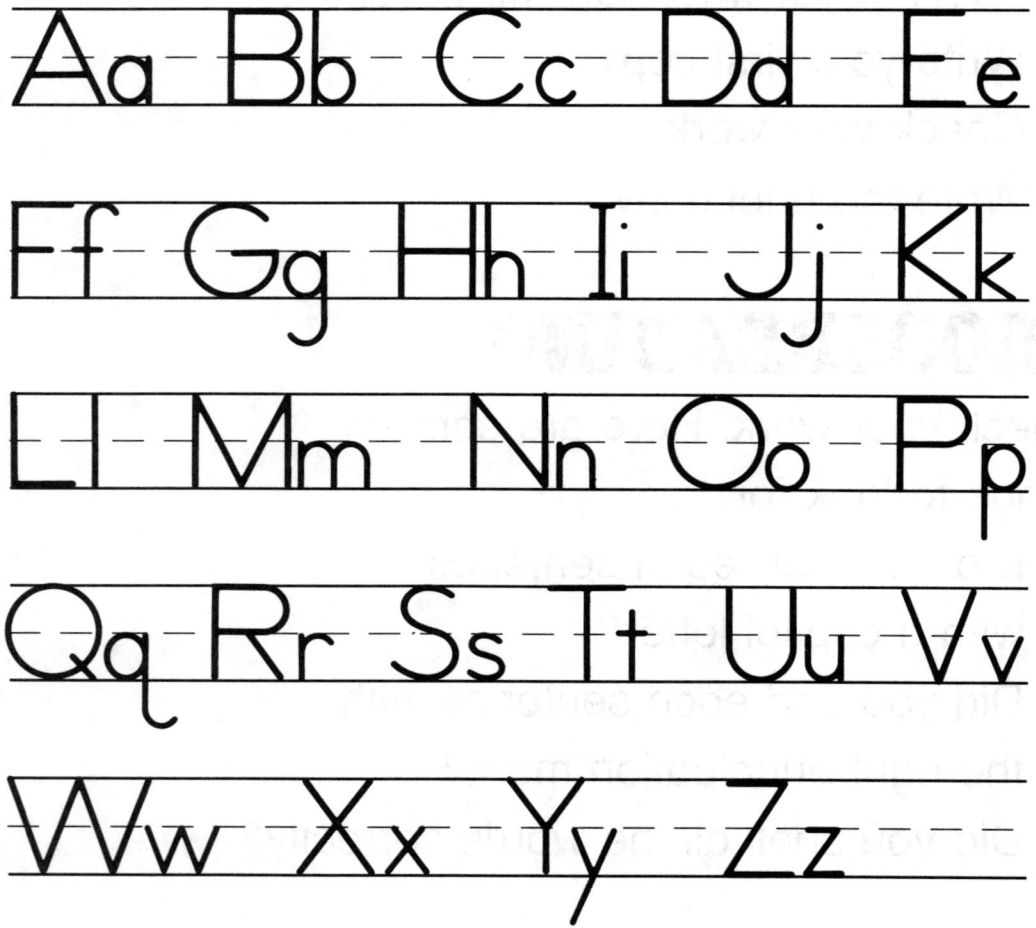

HARD WORDS TO SPELL

Some words are hard to spell. They may not follow spelling rules. The list below shows some of these words. Study them. Learn how to spell them.

are	here	some
come	I	the
do	love	they
for	my	want
from	of	was
have	said	where
her		you

SPELLING PRINCIPLES

17

Short *a*, or /a/, may be spelled *a*.   **cat**

18

Short *o*, or /o/, may be spelled *o*.   **hot**

19

Short *u*, or /u/, may be spelled *u*.   **bug**

20

Short *e*, or /e/, may be spelled *e*.   **get**

21

Short *i*, or /i/, may be spelled *i*.   **pig**

22

The letters *cl* and *fl* spell the sounds at the beginning of some words.   **clap**   **flip**

23

Some words are not spelled as they sound.

        are   **said**

25

Long *a*, or /ā/, may be spelled *a-e*.

        name

26

Long *o*, or /ō/, may be spelled *o* or *o-e*.

        no   **note**

27

Long *e*, or /ē/, may be spelled *e* or *ee*.

        he   **see**

28

Long *i*, or /ī/, may be spelled *i-e*.

        kite

29

Long *a*, or /ā/, may be spelled *ay* or *ai*.

        day   **rain**

31

The letters *sn* and *st* spell the sounds at the beginning of some words.

snake   stop

32

The letters *ch* and *th* spell the sound at the beginning of some words.

chat   this

33

The letters *sh* and *wh* spell the sound at the beginning of some words.

shape   whale

SPELLER DICTIONARY

all / bag

A

all   **1** *All of the children were on the bus.*   **2** *She ate all of the apple.*   **3** *All of us are going to the park.*

am *I am happy that you came to my house. I am going to read a story.*

and   **1** *The apple was big and red.*   **2** *One and one make two.*

are *We are glad we came here. You are playing in my room.* **We say:** *I am, you are, he is, she is, it is, we are, you are, they are.*

ate *She ate her lunch. The dog ate its food.*

B

bag *A bag is used to hold things. My father put my lunch in a brown bag. My new shoes are in the shopping bag.*

bake Will you bake a cake for my birthday?

bee A bee can fly from flower to flower.

beg I had to beg him to give me the book.

big Tigers are very big cats. I live in a big city.

bike I ride my bike to school each day.

black **1** The sky is black at night. **2** The pen on the desk is black.

blue **1** Blue is the color of the sky when it is day. **2** Brad and Maria both have blue eyes.

bone Drink milk if you want strong bones. The dog played with the bone.

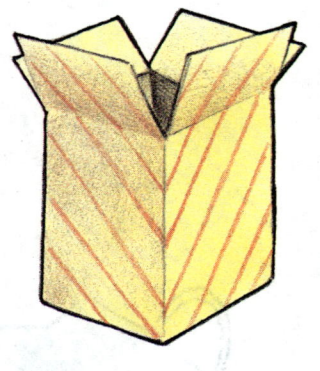

box A box is used to hold other things. This box is made of wood. The children keep their toys in a box.

brown My sister has brown hair. We saw a brown bear in the zoo last week.

bug An ant is one kind of bug. She found a bug in the grass.

bus They ride a bus to school.

but My dog is big, but your dog is small. You may go to the party, but don't stay out after dark.

came / clam

C

came *All of my friends came to my birthday party.*

can¹ **1** *You can swim fast.* **2** *Mom said we can go to the park.* **3** *Can you fix the TV?*

can² *She opened the can of paint. The fish we ate for dinner came in a can.*

cat A cat is a small animal that people keep as a pet. *Our cat likes to drink milk.*

chain **1** *A chain holds my bike to the tree.* **2** *I chain my dog to a tree so it won't run away.*

chase To chase means to go or run after. *Dogs like to chase cats. Do not chase the ball onto the road.*

chat **1** *I like to chat with my friends after school.* **2** *I had a long chat with my sister last night.*

chin Your chin is part of your face. *My father has a cut on his chin.*

chop *Please chop some wood for the fire. Chop the nuts and put them in the cup.*

clam A clam is a kind of animal that lives in water. *We looked for a clam in the sand by the sea.*

clap / dig

clap We will clap our hands when the show is over.

class There are many children in my class at school.

clay There is clay under the sea. He made a cup out of clay.

clip[1] We clip my dog's coat when his hair grows long.

clip[2]   **1** You can hold these papers together with a clip.   **2** Please clip these papers together.

club My club gets together every day after school.

come My dog will come to me when I call his name. All of your friends will come to the park.

cup A cup is something to drink from. I like to drink milk from a cup.

D

dad My dad rides a bus to work every day. My dad and I play ball at the park.

day   **1** The sky is light when it is day.   **2** We had a nice day.

did Did you see that beautiful bird? Yes, I did.

dig Our dog likes to dig for bones in the ground.

160

dime *I got a dime for helping my mom. The man in the store will take my dime.*

do **1** *Please do this work for me.* **2** *Do you like milk?* **3** *She swims better than I do.*

EF

fan **1** *We use a fan in our house when it is hot.* **2** *My aunt has a pretty paper fan.*

feel **1** *You can feel the water by putting your hand in it.* **2** *Kim and Reggie feel happy today.*

feet **1** *We have two feet for walking.* **2** *The girl is three feet tall.*

fin *A fin is a part of a fish that helps it swim. Fish move their fins as they swim.*

fine[1] **1** *Everyone liked the fine food.* **2** *I feel fine today.*

fine[2] *She got a fine because she did not stop at the red light.*

flag *The flag of our country is red, white, and blue. Juan made a flag for our club.*

flap[1] *The flag began to flap in the wind.*

flap[2] *The flap on my tent is open.*

flat / game

flat **1** We like to ride our bikes on a flat road. **2** Our car has a flat tire.

flip Let's flip a dime to see who goes first.

fly¹ A fly is a kind of bug. *The bird ate a little, black fly.*

fly² *We saw the bird fly from one tree to another. I like to fly my kite in the wind.*

for **1** She went for a walk in the park. **2** He worked here for two days. **3** That box is for toys. **4** He will thank you for the book.

fox A fox is a wild animal that looks something like a dog. *The fox ran after the rabbit.*

from **1** We took a train from one city to the next. **2** Please take that book away from him. **3** His hands are blue from the cold.

fun *I had fun at your party. That game was a lot of fun.*

G

game **1** Sarah and Mike will play a game of ball outside. **2** This store has the game that I want for my birthday.

gate If you leave the gate open, the dog will run away.

gave Pat gave me a beautiful flower.

get 1 Did you get my letter? 2 Be sure you get to school on time. 3 It will get cold outside in the winter.

go 1 We can go to the zoo. 2 Cars go on the street. 3 Please do not go until the show is over.

got 1 I got a new coat today. 2 I got tired waiting for you.

gray Gray is a color that is made by mixing black and white. *Grandma has gray hair.*

green Green is the color of grass. 1 *The leaves on that plant are green.* 2 *Bess has green eyes.*

H

had 1 She had a birthday party last night. 2 I had a cold but now I feel better.

have 1 I have a big dog. 2 We have to leave for school now. 3 Please have this room cleaned. 4 Will you have milk or water?

he Mr. Green is old but he still swims fast.

hen / hug

hen We leave seeds for the hen to eat.

her 1 I gave her my book. 2 Have you seen her today? Her dog is in the house.

here 1 I will wait for my mother and my sister right here. 2 The children come here to have fun. 3 Where should I go from here?

hide To hide means to keep from being seen. I'll hide the birthday cake so it will be a surprise. When we play, Jill will hide first.

him I let him ride my bike. Jim wants to go, so take him with you. Give him some milk.

home A home is a place to live. I go home every day after school. My home is at 6 Pine Road.

hop Can you hop on your right foot? Rabbits hop from one place to another as they look for food. We like to sing and hop.

hope I hope you feel better very soon. I hope the rain stops so we can go to the zoo.

hot The sun is very hot. That fire was hot.

hug 1 The little girl wanted to hug my kitten. 2 The boy gave his dad a hug.

I

I *I am six today. I feel fine. I like my new friend.*

in **1** *The dog is in the house. Put the toy in the box.* **2** *It snows in the winter.*

is **1** *She is six.* **2** *Father is not home now. Is that you at the door?*

J

jeep A jeep is a small car. *Tom rides in a jeep because the roads are snowy.*

jet **1** *A jet of water came out of the tap.* **2** *You can fly to another country in a jet.*

joke **1** A joke is something that makes people laugh. *Jeff told a funny joke and everyone laughed.* **2** *At school we joke with our friends.*

KL

kite *My kite is flying in the wind.*

leg **1** *Can you stand on one leg?* **2** *The leg of the chair is white.*

like / my

like¹ 1 My coat is like yours. 2 It is like him to be on time. 3 It looks like it is going to snow. 4 I feel like eating now.

like² 1 Dogs like bones. 2 I like you very much.

love 1 I love my family. He loves his country. 2 I love to read. 3 He has a love for all kinds of animals.

M

made 1 I made a cake for her birthday. 2 It is made of paper.

may 1 May I leave now? May I have some paper? 2 The man said that it may snow today.

me Please give me an apple. My sister takes me to school every day.

mine¹ The hat on the table is mine. The red bike is yours; mine is blue.

mine² 1 My father works in a gold mine. 2 He mines for gold.

mom My mom is a doctor. Ask your mom if you can go to the zoo next week.

my My house is near the park. Ted is my brother. That is my book on the table.

166

N

nail **1** You will need one more nail and some wood to make the dog house. **2** Nail the wood together. **3** There is a nail at the end of each toe.

name **1** My mother's name is Kate. **2** I will name my cat Tiger. Can you name this flower?

net Many fish were in my net. Kim hit the ball over the net.

no **1** Can you come? No, I can't. **2** There is no school today.

not My brother is not home now. It did not rain last night. One and one are two, not three.

note **1** The note told me where to find my mother. Please make a note of this. **2** Please note what I am doing now.

nut The squirrel is eating a nut. The nut fell from the tree.

O

of **1** The top of the table is clean. Many of my friends were at the party. **2** The box is made of paper.

orange / pot

orange 1 *I ate an orange after lunch.* 2 *In the fall some leaves turn orange.*

P

paint 1 *We found a can of red paint in the store.* 2 *Please paint my room blue.*

pet 1 *This dog is my pet.* 2 *We pet the kitten all day.*

pig *A pig is an animal that you may find in the country. My little brother has a toy pig.*

pink Pink is a color that is a mix of red and white. *The flowers I picked are pink.*

play 1 *May we play at your house today? I play ball every day after school.* 2 *I saw a funny play with my family.*

pole *The flag was on top of a tall pole.*

pop 1 *We heard a pop when our car got a flat tire.* 2 *The tire popped with a big noise.* 3 *The clown will pop out of the box.*

pot *My mother cooks food in a big pot. I have a flower pot in my room.*

purple Purple is a color that is a mix of red and blue. *She has purple shoes.*

QR

rain 1 Rain is water that falls from the sky. *The rain made the ground wet.* 2 *It is going to rain today.*

ran *Mike ran all the way to school. The cat ran away from the dog.*

red *Stop at the red light. The red fire truck was on our street.*

ride 1 *I ride my bike to the park. May I ride in your new car?* 2 *We will take a ride into the country.*

rode *He rode his bike over to my house.*

rope 1 *I like to jump with this rope.* 2 *Can you rope these boxes together?*

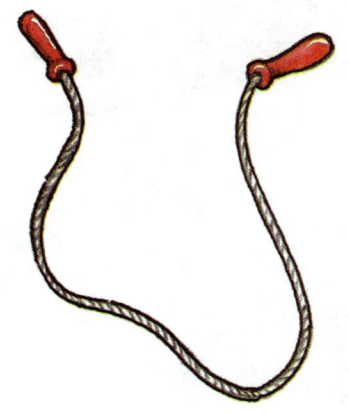

run *My father had to run to catch the bus. You must run for help if you see a fire. That dog likes to run after my ball.*

S

said *Jan said "Hello" to her friend. She said that she would be here soon.*

same / shop

same *Her coat is the same as mine. That is the same girl I saw on the bus. It looks the same as before.*

sat *Mom sat in your chair. I sat in the car all day.*

see **1** *When you close your eyes you cannot see. See that star in the sky.* **2** *I do not see why you must go now.* **3** *Please see who is at the door. See that you do all of your work.*

seed *If you plant this seed in the ground, a flower will grow.*

shape **1** *A box is not the same shape as a ball.* **2** *She was in bad shape after she fell.* **3** *I can shape the clay into a ball.*

shark A shark is a big fish that eats other fish. *Sharks live in the sea. The boat was not near the shark.*

she *My mother says she likes to run. Bess told me she would come to my party.*

shell **1** *My pet turtle has a green shell.* **2** *The shell of this nut is hard to crack.*

ship **1** *A ship is a big boat. I saw the sea from the ship.* **2** *I will ship this box to my friend.*

shop **1** *A shop is a store. I saw a kitten in the pet shop.* **2** *I will shop for a new coat with my mother.*

sit *May I sit on that chair? My leg hurts so I must sit down. My cat likes to sit in the sun.*

size **1** *The two balls are the same size.* **2** *My shoe size is six.*

snail *A snail is a small animal that moves very slowly. Most snails have brown shells on their backs.*

snake *The snake moved slowly along the ground.*

snap **1** *Did you hear the wood on the fire snap?* **2** *The rope may snap if the dog pulls hard.* **3** *The dog may snap at you.* **4** *The box of toys closed with a snap.*

snore *I snore in my sleep when I have a cold. My dad snored all night long.*

snug **1** *It is nice to get into a snug bed on a cold night.* **2** *These shoes are a little too snug.*

some **1** *Some birds cannot sing.* **2** *I can see some of the boys.* **3** *I will keep some and give you the others. Please have some milk before you go.*

stay **1** *Please stay here until I tell you to go. The dog will stay in the house all day. I have no time to stay.* **2** *We came home after a stay with my grandma.*

step / take

step   **1** *I can do that dance step. I was a step from the door when my mother called me.*   **2** *The store is only a step away from your house.*   **3** *I fell down the steps.*   **4** *The man told everyone to step to the back. Don't step on that ant!*

stone   **1** *That house is made of stone.*   **2** *Ben painted a stone.*

stop   **1** *A car must stop at a red light.*   **2** *The rain may stop soon.*   **3** *She asked us to stop making noise.*   **4** *We will stop at the park.*   **5** *The bus made a stop at our school. The bus stop is near my house.*

stove   *My dad cooks food on the stove. This stove burns wood.*

sun   **1** *The sun gives us light.*   **2** *My kitten likes to sleep in the sun.*   **3** *My sister likes to sun herself on the grass.*

T

tail   **1** *My dog has a long tail.*   **2** *The tail of my kite is red.*

take   **1** *Ann will take the book off the table.*   **2** *My mom and dad take a bus to work.*   **3** *Please take it.*

that Did you see that man? Should I take this coat or that one? That girl is my friend.

the Please close the window. The boy in the car is my brother.

then   **1** The show ended, and then we clapped.   **2** I hope you will do the work by then.   **3** If she did all of the work, then she should get all of the money.

these   **1** I like these shoes.   **2** These are my socks.

they Mark and Matt did not come because they missed the bus. I lost my glasses. Do you know where they are?

this I like this cat. This book is mine, and that book is yours.

those   **1** The children played with those toys.   **2** Those are her books and these are my books.

time   **1** A long time ago people cooked on wood stoves.   **2** What time is it?   **3** We had a good time at your party.

top[1]   We ran to the top of the hill.

top[2] A top is a kind of toy. He watched the top go around.

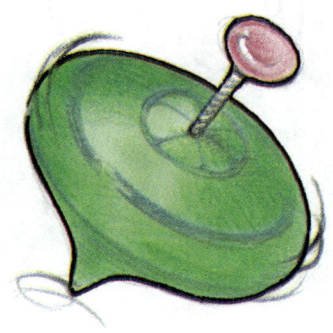

tub Mom filled the tub with water. Sit in that tub until you are clean.

wait / where

UVW

wait   **1** *Wait here until the rain stops. You must wait your turn for the bike.* **2** *There may be a long wait for the bus.*

want *Kim and I want to get a kitten. Do you want more milk?*

was   **1** *I was at her party last night.* **2** *Everyone was singing happy birthday.*   **3** *The food was good.*

web *There was a fly in the web.*

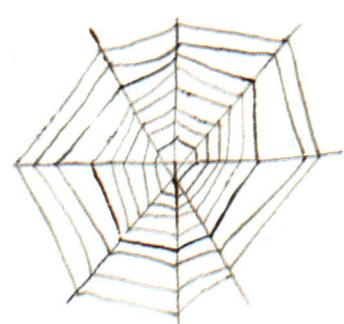

weed   **1** *Please pull that weed out of the ground. That plant is a weed, not a flower.*   **2** *Tim will weed the garden.*

wet   **1** *My coat was wet from the rain.*   **2** *Do not put your hand on the wet paint.*

whale *A whale is a big animal that has the shape of a fish. We saw a whale swimming in the sea.*

when   **1** *When do you start school?* **2** *I will come when you call me.* **3** *We have only three pictures when we need six.*

where   **1** *Where did you put the book? Where does she live?* **2** *Your coat is where you put it.*

which *Which book did you like best? The coat, which I showed you, is very old.*

white *White is the color of snow.* **1** *The paper in this book is white.* **2** *The clean, white snow fell on the ground.*

why **1** *Why did he laugh?* **2** *I don't know why Jill can't come with us.* **3** *Why, look who just got here!*

win *I hope you win the money. The fastest one will win the race.*

XYZ

yellow *Yellow is the color of gold.* **1** *The sun is yellow.* **2** *The old paper has turned yellow.*

yes *Yes, you are right. Yes, you may go to the zoo with Ken.*

you *Do you want to come with me? You push down the top to open the box.*

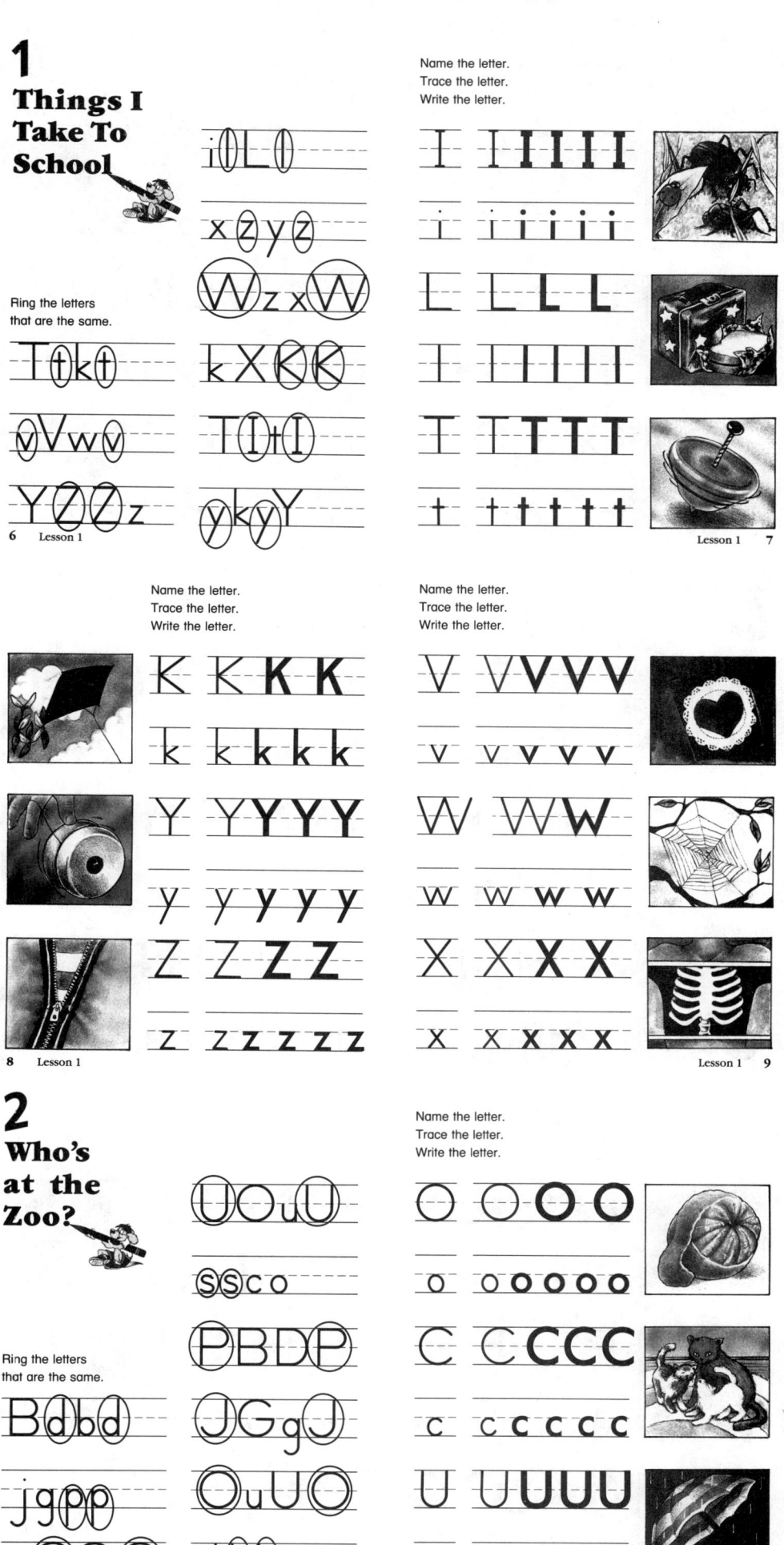

Name the letter.
Trace the letter.
Write the letter.

S S **S S**
s s **s s s**

J J **J J**
j j **j j j**

G G **G G**
g g **g g g**

Name the letter.
Trace the letter.
Write the letter.

P P **P P**
p p **p p p**

B B **B B**
b b **b b b**

D D **D D D**
d d **d d d**

3
Home at Night

Ring the letters that are the same.

ⓜ M n ⓜ
ⓐ e A ⓐ
Ⓔ F e Ⓔ

H Ⓝ Ⓝ M
f F ⓑ ⓑ
ⓞⓞ R F
ⓆⓆ E F
ⓕ r R ⓕ
a ⓠ e ⓠ

Name the letter.
Trace the letter.
Write the letter.

H H **H H**
h h **h h h**

M M **M M**
m m **m m**

N N **N N**
n n **n n n**

Name the letter.
Trace the letter.
Write the letter.

A A **A A**
a a **a a a**

E E **E E**
e e **e e e**

Q Q **Q Q**
q q **q q q**

Name the letter.
Trace the letter.
Write the letter.

F F **F F**
f f **f f f f**

R R **R R**
r r **r r r**

F f R r O o M m

4
My Top Ten Animals

Name the pictures.
Match the beginning sounds.

Name the picture.
Ring the beginning letter.

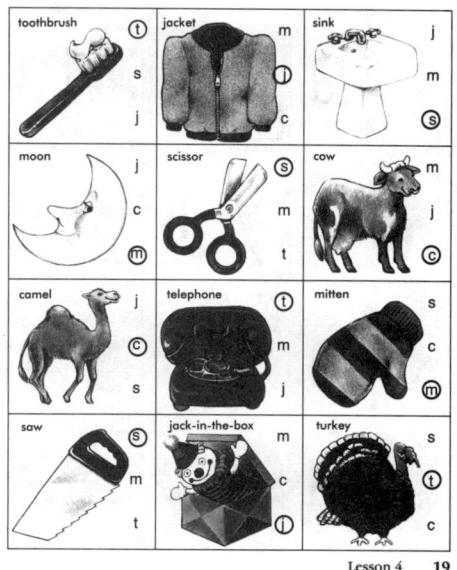

Name the picture.
Write the beginning letter.

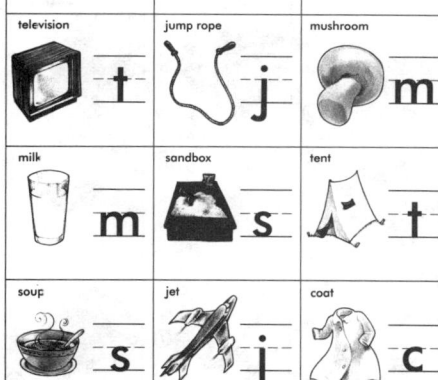

Name the picture.
Write the beginning letter.

5
What Animals Do for Food

Name the pictures.
Match the beginning sounds.

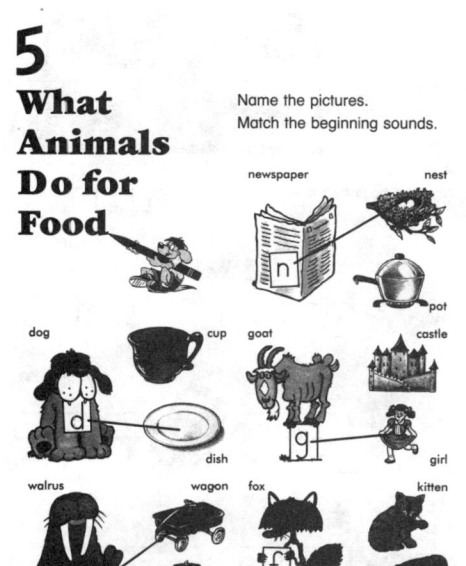

Name the picture.
Ring the beginning letter.

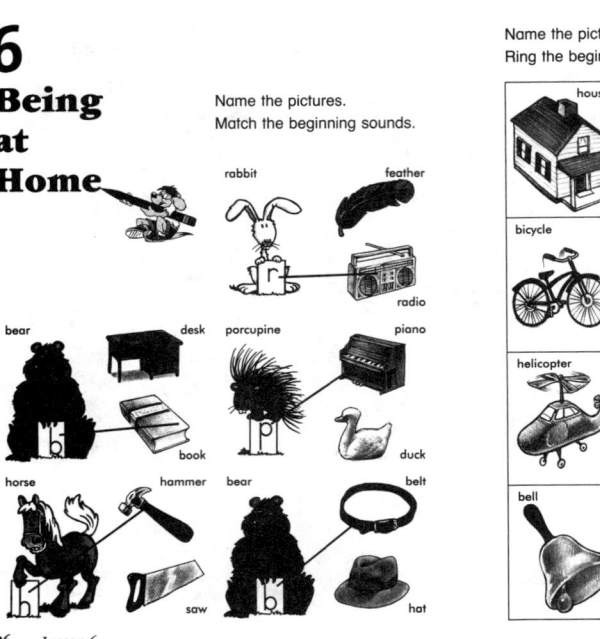
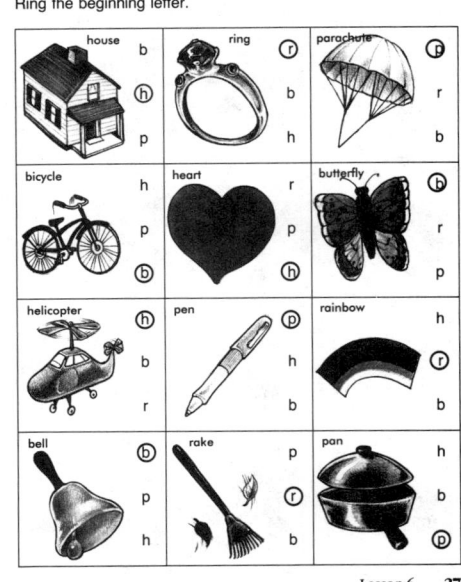

7 Going on Vacation

Name the pictures.
Match the beginning sounds.

Name the picture.
Ring the beginning letter.

Name the picture.
Write the beginning letter.

k l v y z

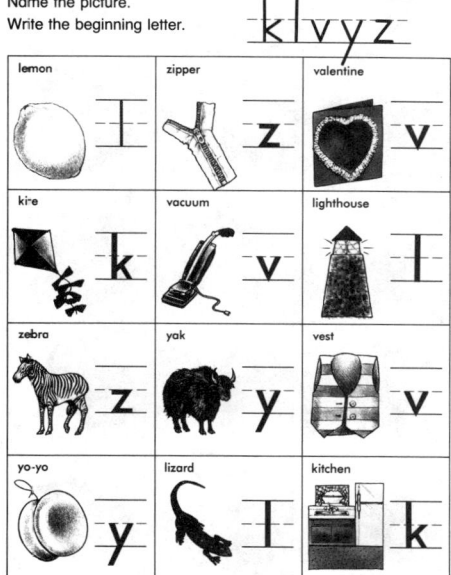

Name the picture.
Write the beginning letter.

k l v y z

yak — yak
kiss — kiss
lid — lid
van — van
zoo — zoo
log — log

8 Winter Treats

Name the pictures.
Match the ending sounds.

Name the picture.
Ring the ending letter.

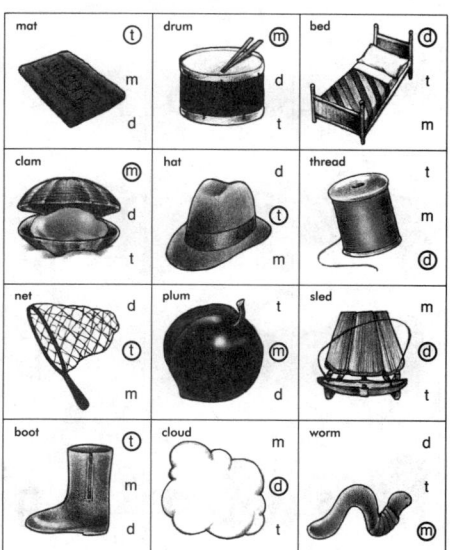

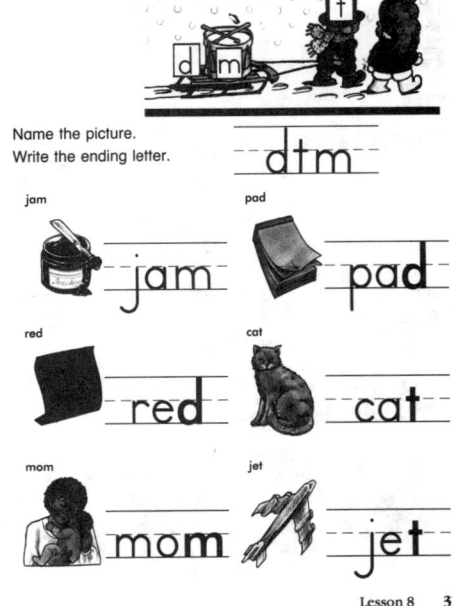

Name the picture.
Listen for the short *a* sound.
Write the letter *a*.

48 Lesson 11

Name the picture.
Write the letter.

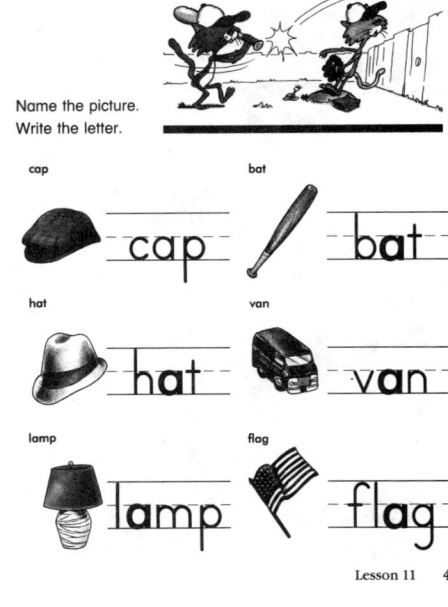

Lesson 11 49

12
Fox and Box

Ring the pictures with the same middle sound as fox

50 Lesson 12

Match the middle sounds.

Lesson 12 51

Name the picture.
Listen for the short *o* sound.
Write the letter *o*.

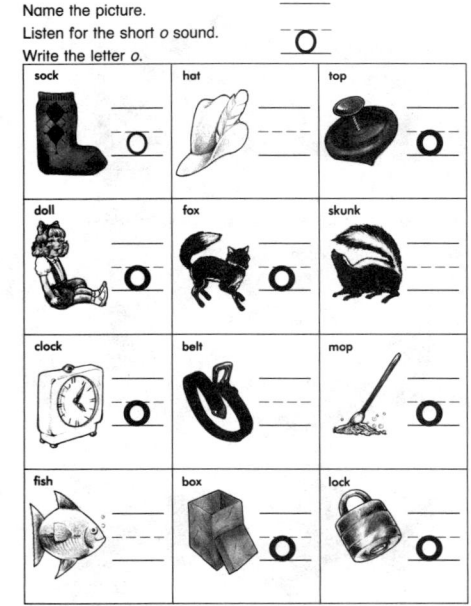

52 Lesson 12

Name the picture.
Write the letter.

Lesson 12 53

13 My Trunk on the Truck

Ring the pictures with the same middle sound as duck

Match the middle sounds.

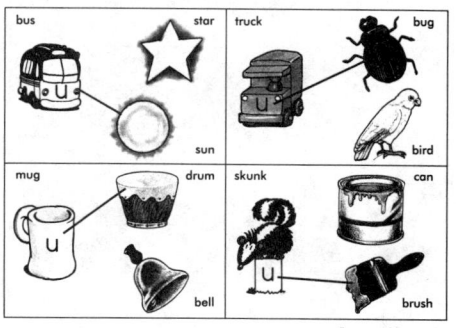

Name the picture.
Listen for the short *u* sound.
Write the letter *u*.

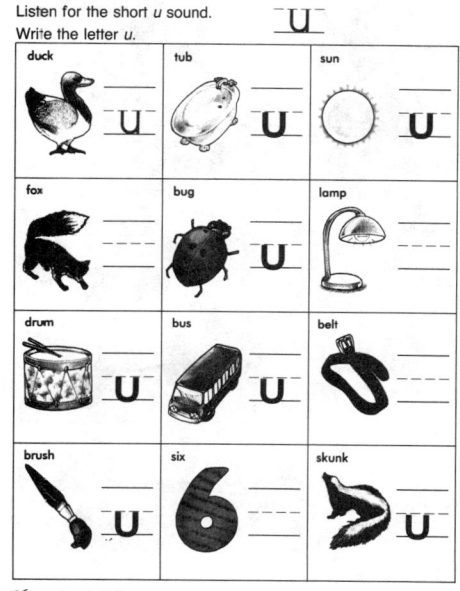

Name the picture.
Write the letter.

14 My Desk at School

Ring the pictures with the same middle sound as hen

Match the middle sounds.

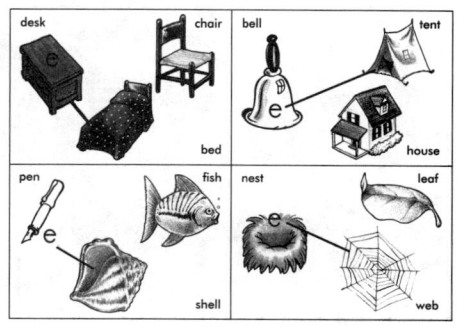

A. Name the pictures.
B. Write the Core Words that rhyme with the picture names.

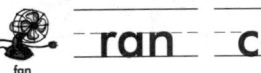
fan — ran   can

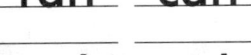
hat — cat   sat

pad — dad

flag — bag

CHALLENGE WORDS

C. Write the Challenge Words where they belong.
Ring the letter that spells short *a* in each word.

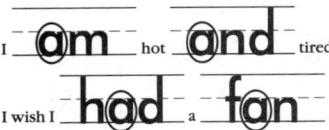
I **am** hot **and** tired.
I wish I **had** a **fan**.

72 Lesson 17

WRITE ON YOUR OWN

Write about a race you saw
or a race you ran in.
Spell the words as well as you can.

PROOFREADING PRACTICE

Cross out the six mistakes.
Write the right words on the lines.

My ~~dod~~ runs. He ~~kan~~ run fast. He ~~rin~~ in the park. Then he ~~st~~ down. He opened the ~~bog~~. A small ~~kat~~ jumped out.

dad   ran   bag
can   sat   cat

Now proofread your writing.

CORE		CHALLENGE	
dad	cat	fan	am
ran	sat	had	and
can	bag		

Lesson 17   73

18   Hop on Top

CORE   **Focus**

1. top   top   Say *top* and *box*.
2. box   box   Listen for the middle sound.
3. hop   hop   It is called the short *o* sound.
4. fox   fox   Write *top* and *box*. Ring the letter that spells the short *o* sound.
5. hot   hot   Now do the same with the other words.
6. not   not

CHALLENGE

7. mom   8. pop   9. got   10. pot

74   Lesson 18

WORDS and MEANINGS
Write the missing Core Words.

Fox on a Box

Look at the **fox**.
It is on **top** of the **box**.
Can you **hop** up there, too?
I can **not** do it. I am too **hot**!

• Add the letters *ot* to make words.
  Ring the word that names the picture.

  lot   (cot)   spot

• Add the letters *op* to make words.
  Ring the word that names the picture.

  mop   (shop)

Lesson 18   75

A. Name each picture. Write the Core Word or Words that have the same beginning sound as each picture name.

fan — fox
hat — hop   hot
tiger — top
ball — box
nest — not

CHALLENGE WORDS

B. Write the Challenge Words that begin and end the same.

Here are my **mom** and **pop**.

C. Write the Challenge Words that rhyme.

They have **got** a **pot**.

76   Lesson 18

WRITE ON YOUR OWN

Do you like to hop?
Write about what you do.
Spell the words as well as you can.

DICTIONARY WORKOUT

a b c d e f g h i j k l m n o p q r s t u v w x y z
Trace the letters.
Write the missing letters.

a   b   c   d
m   n   o   p   q   r
u   v   w   x   y   z

Now proofread your writing.

CORE		CHALLENGE	
top	fox	mom	got
box	not	pop	pot
hop	hot		

Lesson 18   77

19 Run in the Sun

CORE

1. bug bug
2. run run
3. but but
4. sun sun
5. nut nut
6. hug hug

FOCUS

Say *bug* and *run*.
Listen for the middle sound.
It is called the short *u* sound.
Write *bug* and *run*. Ring the letter that spells the short *u* sound.
Now do the same with the other words.

CHALLENGE

7. bus 8. cup 9. fun 10. tub

Word Play

A. Read each clue. Listen for short *u*. Write two Core Words that rhyme with the words below. Ring the Core Word that names the picture.

cut — but (nut) — nut
rug — (bug) hug   — bug
bun — run (sun) — sun

CHALLENGE WORDS

B. Write the Challenge Word that fits the clue.

Wash in it. Drink from it.
tub cup

Ride in it. Have a good time.
bus fun

WORDS and MEANINGS

Write the missing Core Words.

My Pup

My pup and I __run__ in the __sun__.

My pup finds a __bug__, __but__ it runs away. We sit under a __nut__ tree.

I give my pup a __hug__.

• Add the letters *ug* to make words.

jug mug rug

• Add the letters *ut* to make words.

nut cut shut

WRITE ON YOUR OWN

What do you like to do in the sun? Write about it. Spell the words as well as you can.

PROOFREADING PRACTICE

The first word in a sentence begins with a capital letter. Write the sentence correctly. Use a capital letter.

see the bug run.

See the bug run.

Now proofread your writing.

CORE		CHALLENGE	
bug	sun	bus	fun
run	nut	cup	tub
but	hug		

20 A Pet Hen

CORE

1. pet pet
2. hen hen
3. get get
4. net net
5. wet wet
6. leg leg

FOCUS

Say *pet* and *hen*.
Listen for the middle sound.
It is called the short *e* sound.
Write *pet* and *hen*. Ring the letter that spells the short *e* sound.
Now do the same with the other words.

CHALLENGE

7. beg 8. jet 9. web 10. yes

WORDS and MEANINGS

Write the missing Core Words.

A Wet Hen

How did you __get__ so __wet__?

My __pet__ __hen__ ran out in the rain.

Her __leg__ was stuck in a __net__.

• Add the letters *en* to make words.

Ten men sat in a lion's den.

• Add the letters *et* to make words.

I have not met them yet.

A. Name the pictures. Write the Core Word that has the same beginning sound as each picture name. Use *e* to spell the short *e* sound.

heart	hen	wagon	wet
nest	net	goat	get
lamp	leg	pig	pet

CHALLENGE WORDS

B. Write the Challenge Word that goes with each clue.

| a spider's home | web | ask | beg |
| a plane | jet | not no | yes |

84 Lesson 20

Think of a pet you would like to have. Write about it. Spell the words as well as you can.

DICTIONARY WORKOUT

Words in a dictionary are in ABC order.

a b c d e f g h i j k l m n o p q r s t u v w x y z

Write the missing letters below.

a bcd ef gh ijkl

m no pq rs tuv wx yz

Now proofread your writing.

CORE		CHALLENGE	
pet	net	beg	web
hen	wet	jet	yes
get	leg		

Lesson 20 85

21 Did Pig Win?

CORE

1. pig pig
2. win win
3. did did
4. big big
5. in in
6. sit sit

Say *pig* and *win*. Listen for the middle sound. It is called the short *i* sound.

Write *pig* and *win*. Ring the letter that spells the short *i* sound.

Now do the same with the other words.

CHALLENGE

7. dig 8. fin 9. him 10. is

86 Lesson 21

Write the missing Core Words.

A First Prize Hat

My pet <u>pig</u> won first prize <u>in</u> a show. What <u>did</u> she <u>win</u>? She won a <u>big</u> hat.

I hope she does not <u>sit</u> on it!

• Add the letters *it* to make words.

fit   hit   lit

• Add the letters *id* to make words. Ring the word that names the picture.

kid   hid   (lid)   lid

Lesson 21 87

A. Name each picture. Write the Core Words that rhyme with each picture name.

| wig | pig | | big |
| grin | win | | in |

B. Name each picture. Write the Core Word that has the same beginning sound as each picture name.

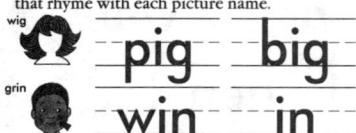

| dog | did | sun | sit |

CHALLENGE WORDS

C. Put the letters in order to spell Challenge Words. Write the Challenge Words.

| i n f | fin | g i d | dig |
| s i | is | i m h | him |

88 Lesson 21

What does a pig look like? What does a pig do? Write about pigs. Spell the words as well as you can.

PROOFREADING PRACTICE

A sentence that asks a question ends with a question mark. Write the sentence correctly. Use a question mark.

Did the pig win.

Did the pig win?

Now proofread your writing.

CORE		CHALLENGE	
pig	big	dig	him
win	in	fin	is
did	sit		

Lesson 21 89

22 Club Flip Flop

CORE

1. clam   clam
2. flip   flip
3. clap   clap
4. flag   flag
5. club   club
6. flat   flat

CHALLENGE

7. class   8. clip   9. flap   10. fly

Words and Meanings
Write the Core Words that go with the pictures.

flag — clam
clap — flat
flip — club

• Add the letters *at* to make words. Ring the word that names the picture. (hat)

hat   mat   bat

• Add the letters *ap* to make words. Ring the word that names the picture. (lap)

lap   tap   nap

Word Play

A. Name the picture. Write the Core Words that have the same beginning sound as the picture name. (flower)

flip   flag   flat

B. Write the Core Words that begin with *cl.*

clam   clap   club

CHALLENGE WORDS

C. Write the Challenge Word that fits each clue. Ring that letters that spell the two beginning sounds.

rhymes with *glass* — class
what birds and jets do — fly
to cut off the ends — clip
the door of a tent — flap

Write On Your Own

Make up a club for you and your friends. Write about your club. Spell the words as well as you can.

DICTIONARY WORKOUT

Words in a dictionary are in ABC order.
a b c d e f g h i j k l m n o p q r s t u v w x y z
Write the words below in ABC order.

boys   dig   can   all

1. all   3. can
2. boys   4. dig

Now proofread your writing.

CORE		CHALLENGE	
clam	flag	class	flap
flip	club	clip	fly
clap	flat		

---

23 You Are You

CORE

1. are   are
2. said said
3. all   all
4. I   I
5. you   you
6. the   the

CHALLENGE

7. here   8. love   9. of   10. was

Words and Meanings
Write the missing Core Words.

A Zoo Trip

Our class went to ___the___ zoo.

"I am glad to see ___you___," ___said___ the man. "Where ___are___ you going?"

"We are going ___all___ over the zoo," we said.

• Add *s* to make words that mean more than one.

hat — hats

cats   mops   pigs
legs   bugs   pets

A. Name each picture. Write the Core Words that rhyme with the picture names.

ball — all   bed — said   zoo — you

B. Write the Core Words that sound like the names of these letters.

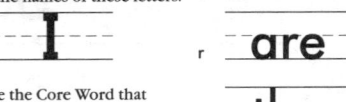

i — I   r — are

C. Write the Core Word that begins with the letters *th*.

the

CHALLENGE WORDS

D. Find the letters that spell the Challenge Words. Ring the letters. Write the Challenge Words.

mn(of)ycyt — of

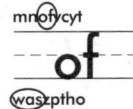

dx(love)fg — love   bac(here) — here   was(was)ptho — was

96 Lesson 23

Who are you? Tell about yourself. Spell the words as well as you can.

PROOFREADING PRACTICE

Cross out the five mistakes. Write the right words on the lines.

"Look at ~~ol~~ ~~tho~~ flags," ~~sed~~ Dick. "Can ~~u~~ name them?" asked Ann. "There ~~r~~ too many," I said.

all   said   are
the   you

Now proofread your writing.

CORE		CHALLENGE	
are	I	here	of
said	you	love	was
all	the		

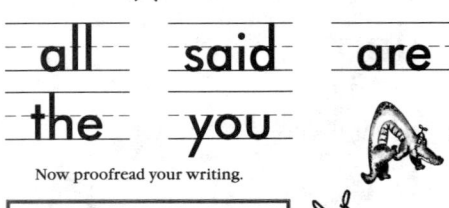

Lesson 23 97

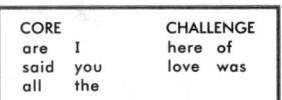 **REVIEW**

LESSON 17 Read the Core Words. Name each picture. Write the Core Word that has the same ending sound as each picture name.

bag
can
dad
sat

bed — dad   pig — bag
sun — can   pot — sat

FOCUS Ring the letter that spells the short *a* sound in each word.

LESSON 18 Read the Core Words. Name each picture. Write the Core Word that has the same beginning sound as each picture name.

fox
hot
top
box

hat — hot   bike — box
fan — fox   table — top

FOCUS Ring the letter that spells the short *o* sound in each word.

98 Lesson 24

REVIEW

LESSON 19 Read the Core Words. Name each picture. Write the Core Word or Words that have the same ending sound as each picture name.

but
bug
run
nut

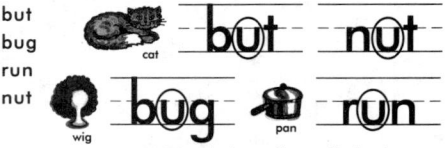

cat — but   nut
wig — bug   pan — run

FOCUS Ring the letter that spells the short *u* sound in each word.

LESSON 20 Read the Core Words. Name each picture. Write the Core Word or Words that rhyme with each picture name.

get
hen
leg
wet

jet — wet   get
ten — hen   egg — leg

FOCUS Ring the letter that spells the short *e* sound in each word.

Lesson 24 99

REVIEW

LESSON 21 Read the Core Words. Name each picture. Write the Core Word that has the same beginning sound as each picture name.

big
did
sit
win

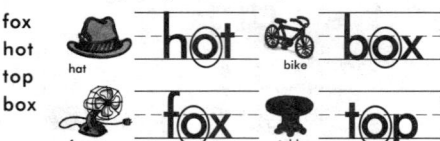

dog — did   seven — sit
wagon — win   bear — big

FOCUS Ring the letter that spells the short *i* sound in each word.

LESSON 22 Read the Core Words. Name each picture. Write the Core Word that rhymes with each picture name.

flag
club
flat
clap

tub — club   bat — flat
map — clap   bag — flag

FOCUS Ring the two letters that spell the beginning sounds in each word.

100 Lesson 24

REVIEW

LESSON 23 Read the Core Words. Name each picture. Write the Core Word that rhymes with each picture name.

all
are
I
said

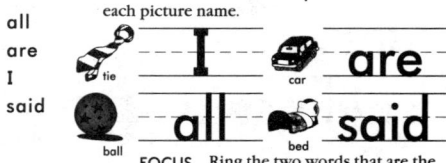

tie — I   car — are
ball — all   bed — said

FOCUS Ring the two words that are the hardest for you to spell.

- Add the letters *ap* to make words. Ring the word that names the picture.

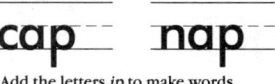

cap   nap   (map)

- Add the letters *ip* to make words. Ring the word that names the picture.

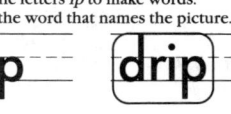
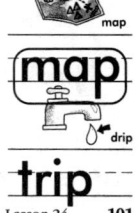

zip   (drip)   trip

Lesson 24 101

25 Make and Bake

CORE

1. made made
2. bake bake
3. name name
4. game game
5. gave gave
6. ate ate

Say *made* and *bake*. Listen for the middle sound. It is called the long *a* sound. The letters *a* and *e* can spell the long *a* sound.

Write *made* and *bake*. Ring the letters that spell the long *a* sound.

Now do the same with the other words.

CHALLENGE

7. take 8. came 9. same 10. gate

102 Lesson 25

WORDS and MEANINGS
Write the missing Core Words.

Baking Bread

My uncle's __name__ is Dave. He likes to __bake__ bread. We __made__ some. Uncle Dave mixed. Then he __gave__ me a turn. It was like a __game__. We __ate__ the bread.

• Add the letters *ake* to make words.

I saw a __snake__ by the __lake__. I began to __shake__.

• Add the letters *ave* to make words.

I was not __brave__. I hid in a __cave__.

Lesson 25 103

Word Play

A. Name each picture. Write the Core Word or Words that have the same beginning sound as each picture name.

nine __name__   book __bake__
apron __ate__   mouse __made__
goat __game__ __gave__

CHALLENGE WORDS

B. Read the words below. Write the Challenge Words that rhyme with them.

ate __gate__   bake __take__
game __same__ __came__

104 Lesson 25

WRITE ON YOUR OWN

Think of a fun thing you would like to make. Write about it. Spell the words as well as you can.

DICTIONARY WORKOUT

Words in a dictionary are in ABC order.
a b c d e f g h i j k l m n o p q r s t u v w x y z
Write the letter that comes after each letter below.

c __d__   i __j__   n __o__
t __u__   x __y__

Write the letter that comes before each letter below.

__b__ c   __g__ h   __h__ i   __p__ q   __w__ x

Now proofread your writing.

CORE		CHALLENGE	
made	game	take	same
bake	gave	came	gate
name	ate		

Lesson 25 105

26 Notes on Bone

CORE

1. go go
2. note note
3. no no
4. home home
5. bone bone
6. rope rope

Say *go* and *note*. Listen for the last sound in *go*. Listen for the middle sound in *note*. It is called the long *o* sound.

The long *o* sound may be spelled *o* or *o_e*.

Write *go* and *note*. Ring the letters that spell the long *o* sound.

Now do the same with the other words.

CHALLENGE

7. hope 8. joke 9. pole 10. rode

106 Lesson 26

WORDS and MEANINGS
Write the missing Core Words.

Visiting Pat

I tied a __rope__ to the wagon. Rover put his __bone__ in the wagon. We will __go__ to see Pat. Then I will take Rover __home__.

• Read the clues. Write the Core Words that match them.

not yes __no__   a little letter __note__

• Add the letter *s* to make words that mean more than one.

__homes__ __bones__ __ropes__
__games__ __notes__ __names__

Lesson 26 107

A. Write the Core Word that rhymes with each picture name.

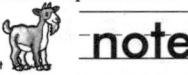 

 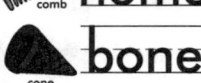

B. Write the Core Word that has the same beginning sound as each picture name. Use words with long o spelled o.

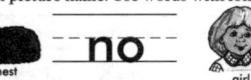

CHALLENGE WORDS

C. Write the Challenge Word that begins like each picture name.

Think about a time in the past. What was it like? Write about this time. Spell the words as well as you can.

PROOFREADING PRACTICE
Cross out three spelling mistakes. Write the right words on the lines.

I came h~~om~~ from school.
Rover wanted to g~~ow~~ for a walk.
He wanted to find his b~~on~~.

 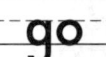 

Now proofread your writing.

CORE		CHALLENGE	
go	home	hope	pole
note	bone	joke	rode
no	rope		

---

27 See Me Weed

CORE

1.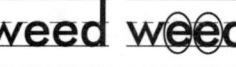
2.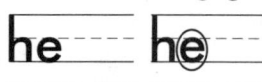
3.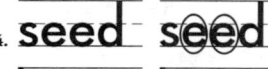
4.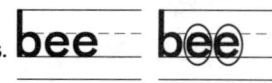
5.
6. see see

> Say *me* and *weed*.
> Listen for the last sound in *me*.
> Listen for the middle sound in *weed*. It is called the long e sound.
> The long e sound may be spelled e or ee.
> Write *me* and *weed*. Ring the letters that spell the long e sound.
> Now do the same with the other words.

CHALLENGE

7. she   8. feel   9. feet   10. jeep

A Bee Sting

Dad gave ___me___ an apple ___seed___.

Then ___he___ pulled up a ___weed___. But

he did not ___see___ the ___bee___. Ouch!

• Add the letters *eed* to make words.

• Add the letters *eep* to make words.

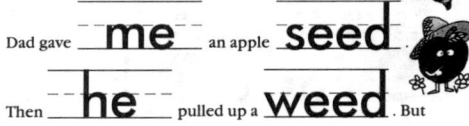

• Ring the word that names the picture.

A. The long e sound can be spelled e. Write the Core Word that has the same beginning sound as each picture name.

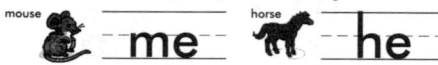

B. The long e sound can be spelled ee. Write the Core Word or Words that have the same beginning sound as each picture name.

CHALLENGE WORDS

C. Ring the four words that do not belong. Then write the Challenge Words that rhyme with them.

Did ~free~ miss the ~sheep~?
Her ~feet~ will ~peel~ very hot.

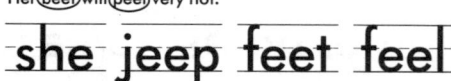

What kind of garden would you like? Write about it. Spell the words as well as you can.

DICTIONARY WORKOUT

Words in a dictionary are in ABC order.

a b c d e f g h i j k l m n o p q r s t u v w x y z

Write the words in ABC order.

see feet he bee weed me

 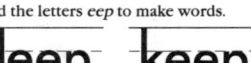 

Now proofread your writing.

CORE		CHALLENGE	
me	seed	she	feet
weed	bee	feel	jeep
he	see		

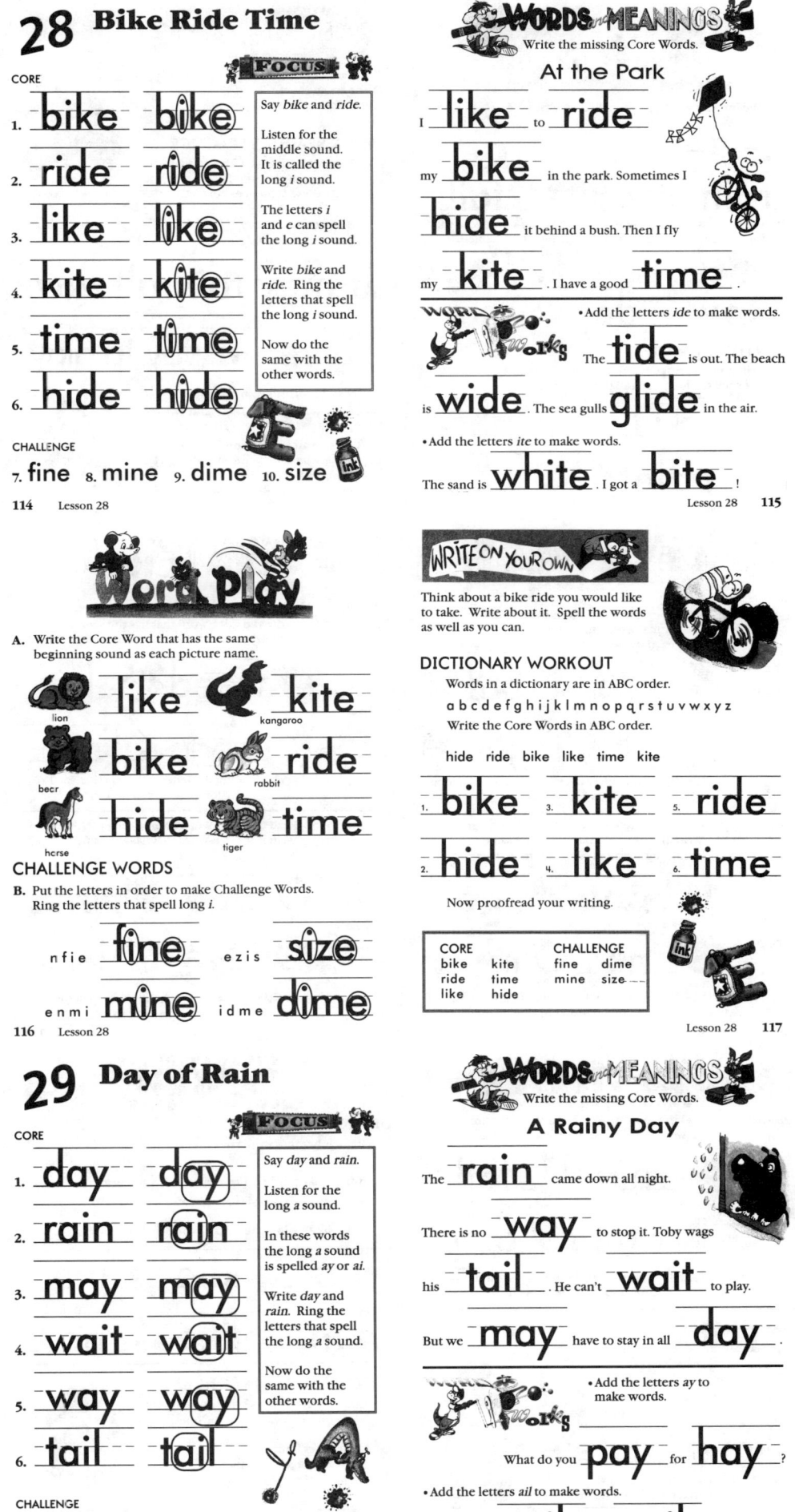

A. The long *a* sound can be spelled *ai*. Write the Core Word that rhymes with each picture name.

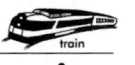  

rain   wait   tail

B. The long *a* sound can be spell *ay*. Write the Core Word that has the same beginning sound as each picture name.

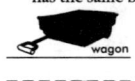  

way   day   may

CHALLENGE WORDS

C. Write the Challenge Words that fit each clue. Ring the letters that spell the long *a* sound in each word.

hammer and **nail**   work and **play**

brush and **paint**   dirt and **clay**

WRITE ON YOUR OWN

What are some nice things about rain?
Write about them.
Check for capitals and periods.

PROOFREADING PRACTICE

A sentence begins with a capital letter.
A telling sentence ends with a period.
Write these sentences correctly.

it may rain all day
there is a way to play

It may rain all day.

There is a way to play.

Now proofread your writing.

CORE		CHALLENGE	
day	wait	nail	clay
rain	way	paint	play
may	tail		

REVIEW

LESSON 25 Read the Core Words. Name each picture. Write the Core Word that rhymes with each picture name.

bake
game
ate
gave

FOCUS Ring the two letters that spell the long *a* sound in each word.

LESSON 26 Read the Core Words. Name each picture. Write the Core Word that has the same beginning sound as each picture name.

go
no
bone
rope

FOCUS Ring the letter or letters that spell the long *o* sound in each word.

REVIEW

LESSON 27 Read the Core Words. Name each picture. Write the Core Word that has the same beginning sound as each picture name.

he
me
see
weed

FOCUS Ring the letter or letters that spell the long *e* sound in each word.

LESSON 28 Read the Core Words. Name each picture. Write the Core Word that has the same beginning sound as each picture name.

bike
kite
ride
time

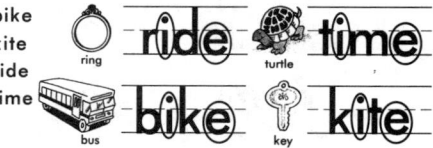

FOCUS Ring the two letters that spell the long *i* sound in each word.

REVIEW

LESSON 29 Read the Core Words. Name each picture. Write the word that rhymes with each picture name.

day
rain
wait
tail

rain   tail
wait   day

FOCUS Ring the two letters that spell the long *a* sound in each word.

• Add the letters *ate* to make words. Ring the word that names the picture.

skate   date   state

• Add the letters *eed* to make words. Ring the word that names the picture.

need   seed   feed

REVIEW

DICTIONARY WORKOUT

Remember that words in a dictionary are in ABC order.

a b c d e f g h i j k l m n o p q r s t u v w x y z

Write the Core Words in ABC order.

kite   like   ate   me   no   bone

1. ate   3. kite   5. me
2. bone   4. like   6. no

PROOFREADING PRACTICE

Cross out the three spelling mistakes.
Write the right words on the lines.

My nam is Stan.
I carry my hom on my back.
It keeps the rane away.

name   home   rain

31 Stop for the Snake

CORE

1. stop stop
2. snake snake
3. snail snail
4. snap snap
5. step step
6. stay stay

FOCUS

Say *stop* and *snake*.

Listen for the first two sounds.

Write *stop* and *snake*. Ring the letters that spell the first two sounds in each word.

Now do the same with the other words.

CHALLENGE

7. snug 8. snore 9. stone 10. stove

WORDS and MEANINGS
Write the missing Core Word.

A Snake on the Path

Ron heard a twig **snap**. He did not **stop** running. He was not slow like a **snail**. He had to **step** over a **snake** on the path. He did not **stay** on the path.

• Add the letters *ug* to make words.

I will help you **tug** the **rug**. Then you give me a **hug**.

• Add the letters *ay* to make words.

Now **may** I go out to **play**?

Word Play

A. Name each picture. Write the Core Words that have the same beginning sounds as each picture name.

snow — snake snap snail

stamp — stop step stay

CHALLENGE WORDS

B. Write two Challenge Words that have the same beginning sounds as *stay* and *stop*.

stone stove

C. Write two Challenge Words that have the same beginning sounds as *snake* and *snail*.

snug snore

WRITE ON YOUR OWN

Think of some good things about snakes. Write about them. Spell the words as well as you can.

DICTIONARY WORKOUT

Words in a dictionary are in ABC order. Many words begin with the same letter. The second letter helps you put them in order.

a b c d e f g h i j k l m n o p q r s t u v w x y z

Write the words in ABC order.

step sun said snail send sock

1. said   3. snail 5. step
2. send   4. sock   6. sun

Now proofread your writing.

CORE		CHALLENGE	
stop	snap	snug	stone
snake	step	snore	stove
snail	stay		

32 This Chat

CORE

1. this this
2. chat chat
3. chop chop
4. that that
5. then then
6. chin chin

FOCUS

Say *this* and *chat*.

Listen for the first sound in each word.

Write *this* and *chat*. Ring the two letters that spell the first sound in each word.

Now do the same with the other words.

CHALLENGE

7. chain 8. chase 9. these 10. those

WORDS and MEANINGS
Write the Core Word that fits each clue.

small talk — **chat**   something over there — **that**

in the past — **then**   part of your jaw — **chin**

something here — **this**   cut into small parts — **chop**

• Add the letters *en* to make words.

men hen then

• Add the letters *in* to make words.

pin win chin

• Ring the words that name the pictures.

Word Play

A. Name each picture. Write the Core Word that ends with the same sound. Use the Core Words that begin with *ch*.

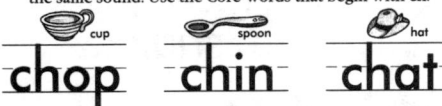

chop chin chat

B. Write the Core Words that end with the same sound as each picture name. Use Core Words that begin with *th*.

this then that

CHALLENGE WORDS

C. Write the Challenge Words that begin the same as *then*.

these those

D. Write the Challenge Words that begin the same as the picture name.

 chase chain

132 Lesson 32

WRITE ON YOUR OWN

What did people do long ago?
How did they go from place to place?
Write about what you think it was like.
Spell the words as well as you can.

PROOFREADING PRACTICE

Cross out the four spelling mistakes.
Write the right Core Words on the lines.

Grandpa and I had a long c~~h~~at. He said, "I planted th~~a~~t tree over there. I was only a boy th~~a~~n. Will you help me plant th~~i~~s new one?"

chat then
that this

Now proofread your writing.

CORE	CHALLENGE
this that	chain these
chat then	chase those
chop chin	

Lesson 32 133

---

33 Which Ship

CORE FOCUS

1. which which
2. ship ship
3. shop shop
4. whale whale
5. when when
6. shape shape

Say *which* and *ship*.

Listen for the first sound in each word.

Write *which* and *ship*. Ring the two letters that spell the first sound in each word.

Now do the same with the other words.

CHALLENGE

7. shark 8. shell 9. where 10. why

134 Lesson 33

WORDS and MEANINGS

Write the missing Core Words.

The Toy Shop

The toy **shop** is on my street. A bell rings **when** you go in. There is a sailing **ship**. There is a gray **whale**. I like the **shape** of it. Do you know **which** one it is?

• Add the letters *ip* to make words.
Ring the word that names the picture.

clip skip   skip

Lesson 33 135

A. Write the Core Words that have the same beginning sound as each picture name.

 sheep

ship shop shape

 whistle

which whale when

CHALLENGE WORDS

B. Write the two Challenge Words that have the same beginning sound as the picture name.

where why   whale

C. Write the two Challenge Words that have the same beginning sound as the picture name.

shark shell   shoe

136 Lesson 33

WRITE ON YOUR OWN

Think of a place you can go on a ship.
Write about the ship and the place.
Spell the words as well as you can.

DICTIONARY WORKOUT

Words in a dictionary are in ABC order.
Many words begin with the same letter.

a b c d e f g h i j k l m n o p q r s t u v w x y z

The second letter of those words tells the ABC order. Write these words in ABC order.

north whale south shape east west

1. east   3. shape   5. west
2. north 4. south   6. whale

Now proofread your writing.

CORE	CHALLENGE
which whale	shark where
ship when	shell why
shop shape	

Lesson 33 137

34 They Have Come

CORE

1. they they
2. have have
3. do do
4. want want
5. her her
6. come come

Say *they* and *have*. Look at how each word is spelled. These words are not spelled the way they sound. You must remember the spelling.

Write the words. Remember the spellings.

CHALLENGE

7. for   8. from   9. some   10. my

138 Lesson 34

WORDS and MEANINGS
Write the missing Core Words.

Animal Fun

Sue ran up to __her__ sister.

I __want__ to see the animals.

__Do__ they __have__ to sleep now?

When are __they__ coming?

Here they __come__ now!

• Add the letter *s* to make words that mean more than one.

shell   shells

__bikes__   __days__   __clams__

Lesson 34 139

Word Play

A. Name each picture. Write the Core Word that rhymes with each picture name.

shoe __do__   tray __they__

B. Name each picture. Write the Core Word or Words that have the same beginning sound as each picture name.

heart __her__ __have__

camel __come__   wig __want__

CHALLENGE WORDS

C. Find the letters that spell the Challenge Words. Ring the letters. Write the words.

sklo(my)s __my__   af(from)p __from__

(for)leng __for__   is(some)l __some__

140 Lesson 34

WRITE ON YOUR OWN

What can you see at a circus?
Write about it.
Spell the words as well as you can.

PROOFREADING PRACTICE

Cross out the six mistakes.
Write the right Core Words on the lines.

When will the animals ca̶g̶e̶? I w̶a̶n̶ to see the lions. Are t̶h̶a̶y̶ all in cages? The elephants h̶a̶y̶ to walk in a row. The band leader spins h̶u̶r̶ baton. I can d̶u̶ that!

__come__   __they__   __her__

__want__   __have__   __do__

Now proofread your writing.

CORE	CHALLENGE
they want	for some
have her	from my
do come	

Lesson 34 141

35 Green Yellow Red

CORE

1. red red
2. black black
3. gray gray
4. green green
5. white white
6. yellow yellow

Say the color words.

Listen for short and long vowel sounds. Look for spellings you have learned.

Write the words. Remember the spellings.

CHALLENGE

7. blue   8. brown   9. orange   10. purple

142 Lesson 35

WORDS and MEANINGS
Look at the picture.
Write the missing Core Words.

Out for a Drive

A __black__ car on a __gray__ street stopped

in front of the __white__ house. The driver wore a

__red__ hat. A big __yellow__ ball

sat on the __green__ grass.

• Add the letters *ed* to make words.
  Ring the word that names the picture.

(bed)   fed   sled

Lesson 35 143

A. Name the pictures. Write the Core Word that has the same beginning sound as each picture.

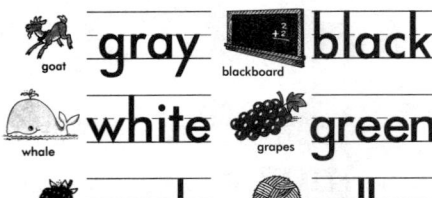

B. Write the Challenge Word that goes with each group.

Write about a garden filled with flowers. Use as many color words as you can. Spell the words as well as you can.

DICTIONARY WORKOUT
A dictionary tells what a word means. Write the word that goes with each meaning.

bed   name   hop   pen

a thing to write with — **pen**   a place to sleep — **bed**

jump up and down — **hop**   what you call someone — **name**

Now proofread your writing.

CORE		CHALLENGE	
red	green	blue	orange
black	white	brown	purple
gray	yellow		

LESSON 31 Remember *sn* in *snap* and *st* in *step*. Read the Core Words. Write the Core Word that rhymes with each picture name.

stop
snake
snail
stay

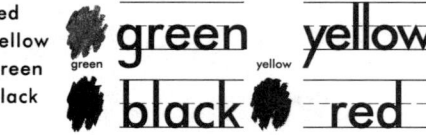

FOCUS   Ring the letters that spell the two beginning sounds in each word.

LESSON 32 Remember *ch* in *chin* and *th* in *this*. Write the Core Word or Words that rhyme with the words below.

chat
chop
that
then

FOCUS   Ring the letters that spell the beginning sound in each word.

LESSON 33 Remember *sh* in *shop* and *wh* in *which*. Write the Core Word that rhymes with the words below.

shape
whale
when
ship

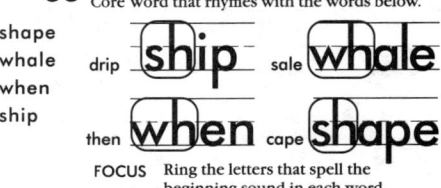

FOCUS   Ring the letters that spell the beginning sound in each word.

LESSON 34 Remember that some words are not spelled the way they sound. Write the Core Word that has the same beginning sound as each picture name.

come
do
have
want

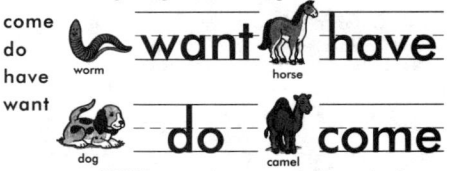

FOCUS   Ring the two words that are hardest for you to spell.

LESSON 35 Remember color words. Name the colors. Write the color words.

red
yellow
green
black

FOCUS   Ring the two color words that you like best.

- Add the letters *ake* to make words. Ring the word that names the picture.

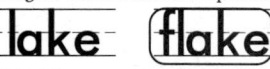

- Add the letters *ame* to make words. Ring the word that names the picture.

DICTIONARY WORKOUT
Many words in the dictionary begin with the same letter. The second letter tells the ABC order.

a b c d e f g h i j k l m n o p q r s t u v w x y z

Write the Core Words in ABC order.

snap   want   shape   stop   which   this

1. shape   3. stop   5. want

2. snap   4. this   6. which

PROOFREADING PRACTICE
Remember that a telling sentence begins with a capital letter and ends with a period. Write the sentence correctly.

we saw a snake

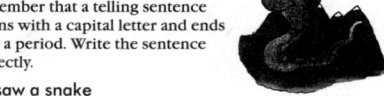

McGRAW-HILL LEARNING MATERIALS
Offers a selection of workbooks to meet all your needs.

Look for all of these fine educational workbooks
in the McGraw-Hill Learning Materials SPECTRUM Series.
All workbooks meet school curriculum guidelines and correspond to
The McGraw-Hill Companies classroom textbooks.

SPECTRUM GEOGRAPHY – NEW FOR 1998!
Full-color, three-part lessons strengthen geography knowledge and map reading skills. Focusing on five geographic themes including location, place, human/environmental interaction, movement and regions. Over 150 pages. Glossary of geographical terms and answer key included.

TITLE	ISBN	PRICE
Grade 3, Communities	1-57768-153-3	$7.95
Grade 4, Regions	1-57768-154-1	$7.95
Grade 5, USA	1-57768-155-X	$7.95
Grade 6, World	1-57768-156-8	$7.95

SPECTRUM MATH
Features easy-to-follow instructions that give students a clear path to success. This series has comprehensive coverage of the basic skills, helping children to master math fundamentals. Over 150 pages. Answer key included.

TITLE	ISBN	PRICE
Grade 1	1-57768-111-8	$6.95
Grade 2	1-57768-112-6	$6.95
Grade 3	1-57768-113-4	$6.95
Grade 4	1-57768-114-2	$6.95
Grade 5	1-57768-115-0	$6.95
Grade 6	1-57768-116-9	$6.95
Grade 7	1-57768-117-7	$6.95
Grade 8	1-57768-118-5	$6.95

SPECTRUM PHONICS
Provides everything children need to build multiple skills in language. Focusing on phonics, structural analysis, and dictionary skills, this series also offers creative ideas for using phonics and word study skills in other language arts. Over 200 pages. Answer key included.

TITLE	ISBN	PRICE
Grade K	1-57768-120-7	$6.95
Grade 1	1-57768-121-5	$6.95
Grade 2	1-57768-122-3	$6.95
Grade 3	1-57768-123-1	$6.95
Grade 4	1-57768-124-X	$6.95
Grade 5	1-57768-125-8	$6.95
Grade 6	1-57768-126-6	$6.95

SPECTRUM READING

This full-color series creates an enjoyable reading environment, even for below-average readers. Each book contains captivating content, colorful characters, and compelling illustrations, so children are eager to find out what happens next. Over 150 pages. Answer key included.

TITLE	ISBN	PRICE
Grade K	1-57768-130-4	$6.95
Grade 1	1-57768-131-2	$6.95
Grade 2	1-57768-132-0	$6.95
Grade 3	1-57768-133-9	$6.95
Grade 4	1-57768-134-7	$6.95
Grade 5	1-57768-135-5	$6.95
Grade 6	1-57768-136-3	$6.95

SPECTRUM SPELLING – NEW FOR 1998!

This series links spelling to reading and writing and increases skills in words and meanings, consonant and vowel spellings and proofreading practice. Over 200 pages in full color. Speller dictionary and answer key included.

TITLE	ISBN	PRICE
Grade 1	1-57768-161-4	$7.95
Grade 2	1-57768-162-2	$7.95
Grade 3	1-57768-163-0	$7.95
Grade 4	1-57768-164-9	$7.95
Grade 5	1-57768-165-7	$7.95
Grade 6	1-57768-166-5	$7.95

SPECTRUM WRITING

Lessons focus on creative and expository writing using clearly stated objectives and pre-writing exercises. Eight essential reading skills are applied. Activities include main idea, sequence, comparison, detail, fact and opinion, cause and effect, and making a point. Over 130 pages. Answer key included.

TITLE	ISBN	PRICE
Grade 1	1-57768-141-X	$6.95
Grade 2	1-57768-142-8	$6.95
Grade 3	1-57768-143-6	$6.95
Grade 4	1-57768-144-4	$6.95
Grade 5	1-57768-145-2	$6.95
Grade 6	1-57768-146-0	$6.95
Grade 7	1-57768-147-9	$6.95
Grade 8	1-57768-148-7	$6.95

SPECTRUM TEST PREP from the Nation's #1 Testing Company

Prepares children to do their best on current editions of the five major standardized tests. Activities reinforce test-taking skills through examples, tips, practice and timed exercises. Subjects include reading, math and language. 150 pages. Answer key included.

TITLE	ISBN	PRICE
Grade 3	1-57768-103-7	$8.95
Grade 4	1-57768-104-5	$8.95
Grade 5	1-57768-105-3	$8.95
Grade 6	1-57768-106-1	$8.95
Grade 7	1-57768-107-X	$8.95
Grade 8	1-57768-108-8	$8.95

Look for these other fine educational series available from McGRAW-HILL LEARNING MATERIALS.

BASIC SKILLS CURRICULUM

A complete basic skills curriculum, a school year's worth of practice! This series reinforces necessary skills in the following categories: reading comprehension, vocabulary, grammar, writing, math applications, problem solving, test taking and more. Over 700 pages. Answer key included.

TITLE	ISBN	PRICE
Grade 3 – new for 1998!	1-57768-093-6	$19.95
Grade 4 – new for 1998!	1-57768-094-4	$19.95
Grade 5 – new for 1998!	1-57768-095-2	$19.95
Grade 6 – new for 1998!	1-57768-096-0	$19.95
Grade 7	1-57768-097-9	$19.95
Grade 8	1-57768-098-7	$19.95

BUILDING SKILLS MATH

Six basic skills practice books give children the reinforcement they need to master math concepts. Each single-skill lesson consists of a worked example as well as self-directing and self-correcting exercises. 48pages. Answer key included.

TITLE	ISBN	PRICE
Grade 3	1-57768-053-7	$2.49
Grade 4	1-57768-054-5	$2.49
Grade 5	1-57768-055-3	$2.49
Grade 6	1-57768-056-1	$2.49
Grade 7	1-57768-057-X	$2.49
Grade 8	1-57768-058-8	$2.49

BUILDING SKILLS READING

Children master eight crucial reading comprehension skills by working with true stories and exciting adventure tales. 48pages. Answer key included.

TITLE	ISBN	PRICE
Grade 3	1-57768-063-4	$2.49
Grade 4	1-57768-064-2	$2.49
Grade 5	1-57768-065-0	$2.49
Grade 6	1-57768-066-9	$2.49
Grade 7	1-57768-067-7	$2.49
Grade 8	1-57768-068-5	$2.49

BUILDING SKILLS PROBLEM SOLVING

These self-directed practice books help students master the most important step in math – how to think a problem through. Each workbook contains 20 lessons that teach specific problem solving skills including understanding the question, identifying extra information, and multi-step problems. 48pages. Answer key included.

TITLE	ISBN	PRICE
Grade 3	1-57768-073-1	$2.49
Grade 4	1-57768-074-X	$2.49
Grade 5	1-57768-075-8	$2.49
Grade 6	1-57768-076-6	$2.49
Grade 7	1-57768-077-4	$2.49
Grade 8	1-57768-078-2	$2.49

THE McGRAW-HILL
JUNIOR ACADEMIC™ WORKBOOK SERIES
AVIALABLE SUMMER 1998

An exciting new partnership between the world's #1 educational publisher and the world's premiere entertainment company brings the respective strengths and reputation of each great media company to the educational publishing arena. McGraw-Hill and Warner Bros. have partnered to provide high-quality educational materials in a fun and entertaining way.

For more than 110 years, school children have been exposed to McGraw-Hill educational products. This new educational workbook series addresses the educational needs of young children, ages three through eight, stimulating their love of learning in an entertaining way that features Warner Bros.' beloved Looney Tunes™ and Animaniacs™ cartoon characters.

The McGraw-Hill Junior Academic™ Workbook Series features twenty books – four books for five age groups including toddler, preschool, kindergarten, first grade and second grade. Each book has up to 80 pages of full-color lessons such as: colors, numbers, shapes and the alphabet for toddlers; and math, reading, phonics, thinking skills, and vocabulary for preschoolers through grade two.

This fun and educational workbook series will be available in bookstores, mass market retail outlets, teacher supply stores and children's specialty stores in summer 1998. Look for them at a store near you, and look for some serious fun!

TODDLER SERIES
32-page workbooks featuring the Baby Looney Tunes™

	ISBN	PRICE
My Colors Go 'Round	1-57768-208-4	$2.25
My 1, 2, 3's	1-57768-218-1	$2.25
My A, B, C's	1-57768-228-9	$2.25
My Ups & Downs	1-57768-238-6	$2.25

PRESCHOOL SERIES
80-page workbooks featuring the Looney Tunes™

	ISBN	PRICE
Math	1-57768-209-2	$2.99
Reading	1-57768-219-X	$2.99
Vowel Sounds	1-57768-229-7	$2.99
Sound Patterns	1-57768-239-4	$2.99

KINDERGARTEN SERIES
80-page workbooks featuring the Looney Tunes™

	ISBN	PRICE
Math	1-57768-200-9	$2.99
Reading	1-57768-210-6	$2.99
Phonics	1-57768-220-3	$2.99
Thinking Skills	1-57768-230-0	$2.99

THE McGRAW-HILL JUNIOR ACADEMIC™ WORKBOOK SERIES - CONTINUED

GRADE 1 SERIES
80-page workbooks featuring the Animaniacs™

	ISBN	PRICE
Math	1-57768-201-7	$2.99
Reading	1-57768-211-4	$2.99
Phonics	1-57768-221-1	$2.99
Word Builders	1-57768-231-9	$2.99

GRADE 2 SERIES
80-page workbooks featuring the Animaniacs™

	ISBN	PRICE
Math	1-57768-202-5	$2.99
Reading	1-57768-212-2	$2.99
Phonics	1-57768-222-X	$2.99
Word Builders	1-57768-232-7	$2.99

SOFTWARE TITLES AVAILABLE FROM McGRAW-HILL HOME INTERACTIVE

The skills taught in school are now available at home! These titles are now available in retail stores and teacher supply stores everywhere.
All titles meet school guidelines and are based on
The McGraw-Hill Companies classroom software titles.

MATH GRADES 1 & 2
These math programs are a great way to teach and reinforce skills used in everyday situations. Fun, friendly characters need help with their math skills. Everyone's friend, Nubby the stubby pencil, will help kids master the math in the Numbers Quiz show. Foggy McHammer, a carpenter, needs some help building his playhouse so that all the boards will fit together! Julio Bambino's kitchen antics will surely burn his pastries if you don't help him set the clock timer correctly! We can't forget Turbo Tomato, a fruit with a passion for adventure who needs help calculating his daredevil stunts.

Math Grades 1 & 2 use a tested, proven approach to reinforcing your child's math skills while keeping them intrigued with Nubby and his collection of crazy friends.

TITLE	ISBN	PRICE
Grade 1: Nubby's Quiz Show	1-57768-011-1	$19.95
Grade 2: Foggy McHammer's Treehouse	1-57768-012-X	$19.95

MISSION MASTERS™ MATH AND LANGUAGE ARTS

The Mission Masters™ -- Pauline, Rakeem, Mia, and T.J. – need your help. The Mission Masters™ are a team of young agents working for the Intelliforce Agency, a high level cooperative whose goal is to maintain order on our rather unruly planet. From within the agency's top secret Command Control Center, the agency's central computer, M5, has detected a threat… and guess what – you're the agent assigned to the mission!

MISSION MASTERS™ MATH GRADES 3, 4 & 5

This series of exciting activities encourages young mathematicians to challenge themselves and their math skills to overcome the perils of villains and other planetary threats. Skills reinforced include: analyzing and solving real world problems, estimation, measurements, geometry, whole numbers, fractions, graphs, and patterns.

TITLE	ISBN	PRICE
Grade 3: Mission Masters™ Defeat Dirty D!	1-57768-013-8	$29.95
Grade 4: Mission Masters™ Alien Encounter	1-57768-014-6	$29.95
Grade 5: Mission Masters™ Meet Mudflat Moe	1-57768-015-4	$29.95

MISSION MASTERS™ LANGUAGE ARTS GRADES 3, 4 & 5 – COMING IN 1998!

This new series invites children to apply their language skills to defeat unscrupulous characters and to overcome other earthly dangers. Skills reinforced include language mechanics and usage, punctuation, spelling, vocabulary, reading comprehension and creative writing.

TITLE	ISBN	PRICE
Grade 3: Mission Masters™ Feeding Frenzy	1-57768-023-5	$29.95
Grade 4: Mission Masters™ Network Nightmare	1-57768-024-3	$29.95
Grade 5: Mission Masters™ Mummy Mysteries	1-57768-025-1	$29.95

FAHRENHEITS' FABULOUS FORTUNE

Aunt and Uncle Fahrenheit have passed on and left behind an enormous fortune. They always believed that only the wise should be wealthy, and luckily for you, you're the smartest kid in the family. Now, you must prove your intelligence in order to be the rightful heir. Using the principles of physical science, master each of the challenges that they left behind in the abandoned mansion and you will earn digits to the security code that seals your treasure.

This fabulous physical science program introduces kids to the basics as they build skills in everything from data collection and analysis to focused subjects such as electricity and energy. Multi-step problem-solving activities encourage creativity and critical thinking while children enthusiastically accept the challenges in order to solve the mysteries of the mansion. Based on the #1 Physical Science Textbook from McGraw-Hill!

TITLE	ISBN	PRICE
Fahrenheit's Fabulous Fortune Physical Science, Grades 8 & Up	1-57768-009-X	$29.95

All titles for Windows 3.1™, Windows '95™, and Macintosh™.

Visit us on the Internet at
www.mhhi.com

STUDENT NOTES

STUDENT NOTES